THE *Quiltmaker* COLLECTION

Quilting Motifs

VOLUME I

A collection of quilting patterns
from QUILTMAKER's first 20 years

By the staff of QUILTMAKER
Edited by Maria Capp
Additional artwork by Annie Segal

PRIMEDIA Consumer Media & Magazine Group
741 Corporate Circle, Ste. A
Golden, Colorado 80401-0101

Additional copies are available for purchase for U.S. $14.95.
Please call 1-800-590-3465 within USA. Outside USA,
phone 720-836-1123 or 303-278-1010.

Editor: Maria Capp
Quilting motif designs: *Quiltmaker* staff
Additional artwork and book design: Annie Segal
Photography: Mellisa Karlin Mahoney

Copyright © 2001 by **PRIMEDIA** Consumer Media & Magazine Group
741 Corporate Circle, Golden, CO 80401

All rights reserved. No part of this book may be reproduced in any form
or by any means without the prior written permission of the publisher,
excepting copies made to adjust motif sizes for personal use only.

First Printing 2001
Manufactured in the United States of America
ISBN: 0-9713713-0-X

Table of Contents

Welcome

How to Use This Book 6

Selecting Motifs 6

Adapting Motifs 7

Marking Your Quilts 7

Marking Tools 8

Positioning Motifs and Using the Variations in this Book 9

Cover Quilt Pattern 82

Index 84

Circle & Angle Templates 88

Charm Tacks™	
Kite	.24
Castle	.24
Double Heart	.25
Butterfly	.25
Snowflake	.30
Reindeer	.30
Twins	.32
Apple Tree	.41
Spinning Top	.53
Swirl	.53
Pie	.53
Rabbit	.54
Turtle	.54
Goose	.71
Cow	.71

Motifs and Variations

Lida Rose	10	Amish Traditions	34	Twirlaway	59
Lady Luck	11	Palace Steps	35	Feather Spray	60
Lantern Lily	12	Chinook	36	Windswept	62
Tulip	13	Camellia	37	Flower of Youth	63
Whirlabout	14	Fanciful Star	38	Furrow Cable	64
Wild Rose	15	Brocade	39	April Love	66
First Bloom	15	Mariner's Star	40	Ivy	67
Strawberry Fields	16	Lemon Twist	42	Coventry	68
Avalon	17	Catch of the Day	42	Soaring Bird	70
Festive Touch	18	Spring Promise	43	Hedgerow	71
Summer Leaves	19	Feathers & Flowers	44	Cloverleaf	72
Thunderbird	20	Floating Clouds & Stars	45	Double Feather Wreath	73
Shasta Daisy	21	Sunshine	45	Butterfly Garden	74
Petite Daisy	21	Ring of Stars	46	Lotus Bud	75
Friendship Blossoms	22	Breezy Blossom	47	Milky Way	75
Bell Blossom	22	Crystal Star	47	Poinsettia	76
Feathered Wreath	23	Hearts in Bloom	48	Bunting & Bows	77
Coleus Leaf	24	Butterflies	50	Monarch	78
Garden Party	25	Scotch Thistle	50	Peach Harvest	78
Leaf Cable	26	White Dove	52	Rosebush	79
Corona	27	Lacy Lock	53	Whirlwind	79
Leaf Trail	28	Irish Cable	54	Autumn Breeze	80
Sundae Surprise	29	Floating Lily	55	Hearts Aflutter	80
Gift Wrap	30	Love's Bloom	56	Continuous Cable	81
Star Bound	32	Cupid's Arrow	57	Ribbon Reel	81
Zinnia	33	Fond Memories	58		

THE *Quiltmaker* COLLECTION ▪ *Quilting Motifs* ▪ 5

Welcome

Welcome to Volume 1 of *The QUILTMAKER Collection: Quilting Motifs.* For many years, our magazine has been trusted for clear and accurate step-by-step directions for making a quilt – from start to finish. This includes beautiful quilting motifs to enhance your patchwork or applique, and more recently beautiful continuous-line quilting motifs for the ever-increasing number of machine quilters. This volume represents a variety of motif styles and sizes spanning QUILTMAKER'S 20 years in publication. Many variations on each motif provide ideas and alternatives for every project. And for those with specific requirements, we include an exhaustive index allowing you to search for a motif based either on a theme or the size of space requiring quilting.

We hope you find this collection an invaluable and inspiring resource as you select the perfect designs to create the rich surface textures of your quilt.

How to Use This Book

Please note that the measurements for the quilt blocks and borders are finished sizes into which the motifs can fit. Seam allowances are already hidden by the time you get to the quilting step.

To find a motif to fit a specific space, see the size index for our suggestions.

Refer to the Table of Contents if you have a themed quilt and want flower, holiday, bird or even food motifs.

When you need quilting inspiration, just leaf through the pages.

Selecting Motifs

Answering these questions will help narrow down motif possibilities.

What is the style of my quilt?
For a formal, traditional quilt, look for circular motifs, feathers

or flowers. You can enhance the formal style of your quilt by centering motifs on each plain block.

If you're working for an informal or scrappy look, less defined shapes work well. You may want to place motifs randomly or use a combination of motifs in different areas to enhance the style.

Do I want to enhance or contrast the lines of the quilt top?
If your quilt is made up of diagonals that you want to enhance, choose an angular, geometric motif. If you want to soften the appearance of the diagonal lines, choose a gentler and more rounded motif.

What size space do I need to fill?
Our size index will help you find a motif to fit your space. If the motif you choose doesn't have an option that fits, see "Adapting Motifs" on page 7.

Does the space I need to fill have a busy print or a plain print?
Solid fabric is the perfect place to showcase the intricate quilting motifs you love. The same motif on a busy print fabric will get lost, and all your quilting will go unnoticed.

Am I machine quilting or hand quilting?
Hand quilting allows most any kind of design without limitations. Make sure you find a motif that will showcase all the time you put into the quilting.

If machine quilting is your method of choice, you may want to start in the subject index with continuous-line patterns. You can begin and finish these individual motifs without having to start and stop sewing. If you don't select a continuous-line pattern, keep in mind that you will have to begin and end the line wherever it dead-ends. Make sure to start and stop these lines with tiny stitches to prevent them from pulling out.

How accomplished am I as a quilter?
If the thought of quilting even one of those detailed motifs strikes fear in your heart, choosing it for your queen-sized quilt project will only mean that the quilt never gets done. Choose something simpler that you will be happy with, saving the detailed motif for a pillow top that requires only one design. If you love to quilt and can't wait to tackle the biggies, go for it!

Adapting Motifs

You've found a motif you love, but for one reason or another it isn't exactly right. Here are some ways to work with the motif you can't live without.

Change the size

The easiest way to adjust the size of a motif is with a photocopy machine. First, make a paper shape that represents the patch for the motif. Then reduce or enlarge the motif on the copier until it fits into the paper shape. Layering the two papers and holding them up to a light is a good way to check.

Consider an alternative placement

Who says a motif has to fit inside a block? If your motif is too large, perhaps it can break the boundaries of the block and overlap into other areas of the quilt. If it fits the style of the quilt, why not?

If your motif is too small, consider multiples in the same block, or randomly place them over the surface of the quilt. This is especially effective with leaves, small flowers or stars that scatter randomly in nature just as they can on your quilt.

Consider filling in the space with other quilting

If your motif is small and you don't want multiple shapes but need more quilting, use another method to fill in the space.

For a formal look, add a grid of quilting behind the motif.

Machine stipple all around the motif to cover areas quickly and make the motif stand out.

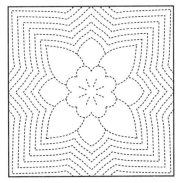

Echo quilt around the motif to give your quilt an informal, casual look.

Marking Your Quilts

Marking for hand quilting

- A light pencil line is often all you need. The line will be covered by the quilting thread, and little or no erasing is necessary.
- If you are quilting ¼" from seam allowances, consider using tape as described in the **Marking Tools Table** on page 8.
- Most hand quilters mark quilts before basting.

Marking for machine quilting

- The line must be clearly visible to make the machine's path easy to follow.
- When you trace a motif, plan the path the machine will take. This will give you some practice before actually quilting.
- Tracing paper, contact paper and freezer paper are all great alternatives to marking your quilt. See the **Marking Tools Table** on page 8 for more information.

Making templates

To make a template for a marking technique that requires tracing, you will need heavy clear plastic. Trace the motif on the plastic using a permanent marker. If the design is closed, simply cut on the marked outer line. For a more intricate motif, use an X-Acto® knife to cut out the lines, cutting a wide enough channel to accommodate your marking tool. You can also buy a double-bladed knife made specifically for cutting channels.

Marking tools

Every quilter will have her favorite way of marking a quilt for one reason or another.
This table helps you identify tools to find your own preferences.

Product	Description	Type of Quilting	Pros	Cons	Requires a template?
Pencil	Quilter's colored pencils Mechanical pencils	Hand	Thin line usually disappears under stitching Easily erased	Often not dark enough to be seen for machine quilting	yes
Chalk	Tailor's chalk Chalk dispensers Chalk pencils	Hand/ Machine	Comes in a variety of colors Erases easily with rubbing	Can rub off before you want it to	yes
Soap	Soapstone Soap slivers	Hand	Easily washed out Economical Shows well on dark fabrics	Often not dark enough to be seen	yes
Markers	Air-erase markers Washable markers	Hand/ Machine	Good dark line	Some quilters worry about marks reappearing	yes
Hera marker	Tool that "creases" the quilt to show markings	Hand/ Machine	Makes no permanent mark	Can be difficult to see Can wear off before you want it to	yes
Tape	Masking tape Narrow tape with marked lines	Hand/ Machine	Peels off easily Marking of the quilt top is not necessary Can be reused	Only for straight lines or very gentle curves	no
Quilter's guide on machine	Bar attaches to the walking foot on some machines	Machine	Marking of the quilt top is not necessary	Best for straight lines with a guide to follow	no
Tracing paper	Motif is traced on the paper and pinned to quilt top	Machine	Marking of the quilt top is not necessary	Motif must be traced on every sheet	no
Contact paper, Freezer paper	Motif is traced on paper and cut out, then stuck to quilt	Machine	Reuseable several times Marking of the quilt top is not necessary	For outline design only If stitches puncture paper, can be difficult to remove	no

Positioning Motifs and Using the Variations in This Book

Finding the Center

For a centered single motif, find the center of the block or patch by folding the fabric in half lengthwise and then crosswise and lightly finger pressing. When unfolded, the creases will help you center the motif for tracing.

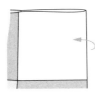

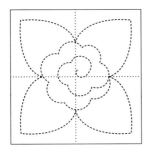

Finding Diagonal Lines

Many variations are lined up with diagonal lines. To find these, cut a piece of tracing paper to the size of the finished block or patch. Fold in half from corner to corner, then fold in half again. When unfolded, the creases can be used to line up motifs to create the whole design.

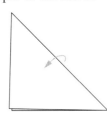

Finding Horizontal and Diagonal Lines

To recreate some designs, you may need to add a horizontal or diagonal line. Fold the paper lengthwise and crosswise, then open it out and refold it corner to corner to get horizontal, vertical and diagonal lines to line up the motifs.

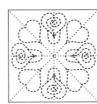

Eight-Point Circles

Some design options use a circle to lay out the motifs. A ¼-circle template is on page 88. The template includes all the circle sizes used in this book. To draw a circular motif, first find the center of your tracing paper by folding. Next, open up the paper, align the center marks, and trace the arc. Then, rotating the paper ¼ turn each time, repeat until you have a complete circle.

For example, one of the 11½" blocks for the Rosebush motif on page 79 has eight leaves evenly spaced around an 8½" circle. To draw this design, place a dot where each fold crosses the circle. Line up

the leaf motif with the dots, trace, and repeat until the circle of leaves is complete.

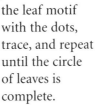

Six-Point Circles

Another variation for the Rosebush motif uses only six leaves. To draw this design, draw the circle as before, then use the angle template on page 88 to draw lines at 60° angles, as shown.

Place a dot where each line crosses the circle and line up the motif

between the dots. Trace the leaf, then rotate and repeat until the circle of leaves is complete.

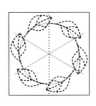

Another example of a six-point circle is a variation of the Ivy motif on page 67. Draw a 4½" circle and mark lines at 60° angles as shown. Place three dots on the circle; one at every other intersection of the lines and the circle.

Starting at each dot, trace the partial Ivy motif three times. In this case, the circle

becomes part of the quilting design. Be sure to trace it when transferring the design to the quilt top.

Lida Rose

Some layouts require the "tucked in" leaf shown here in gray.

For border, flip every other motif and match dots. Reversed motifs are shown in gray.

Lady Luck

Lantern Lily

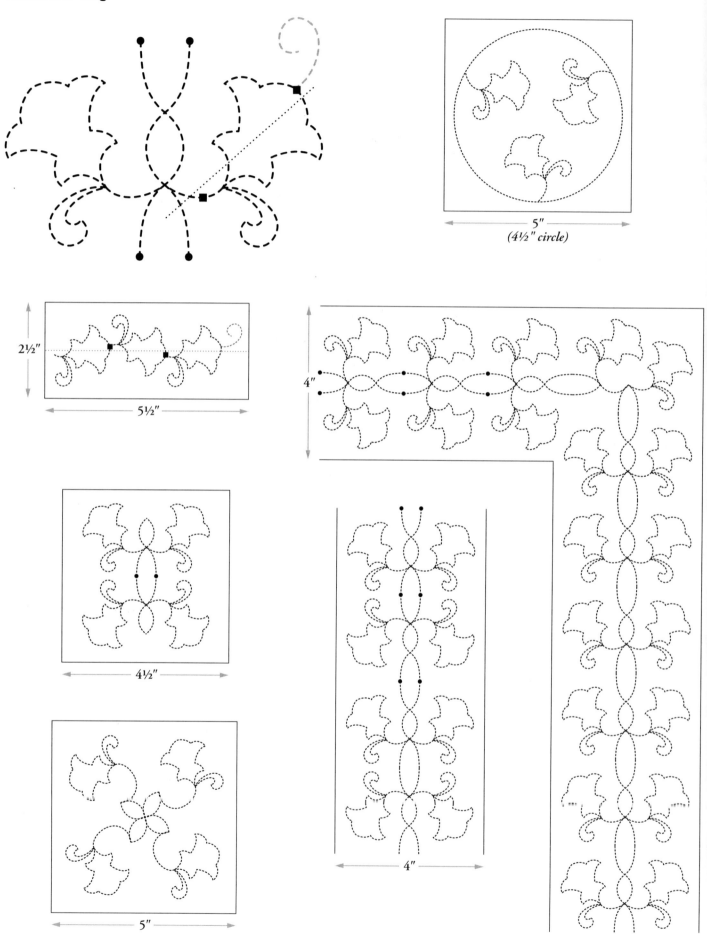

12 ■ THE *QUILTMAKER* COLLECTION ■ *Quilting Motifs*

Tulip

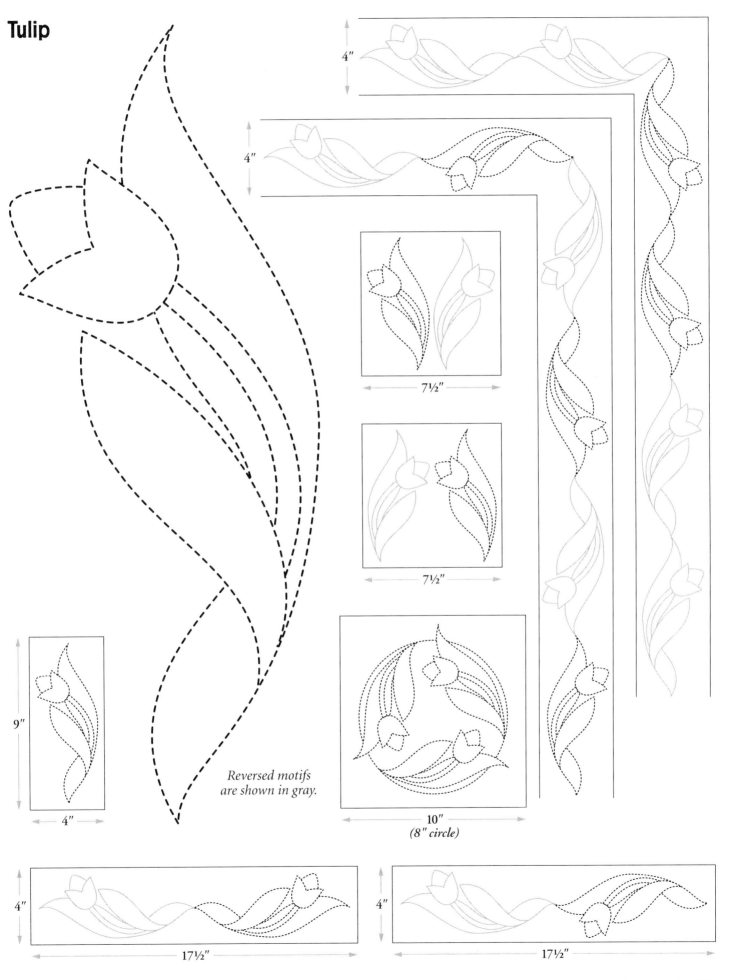

Reversed motifs are shown in gray.

Whirlabout

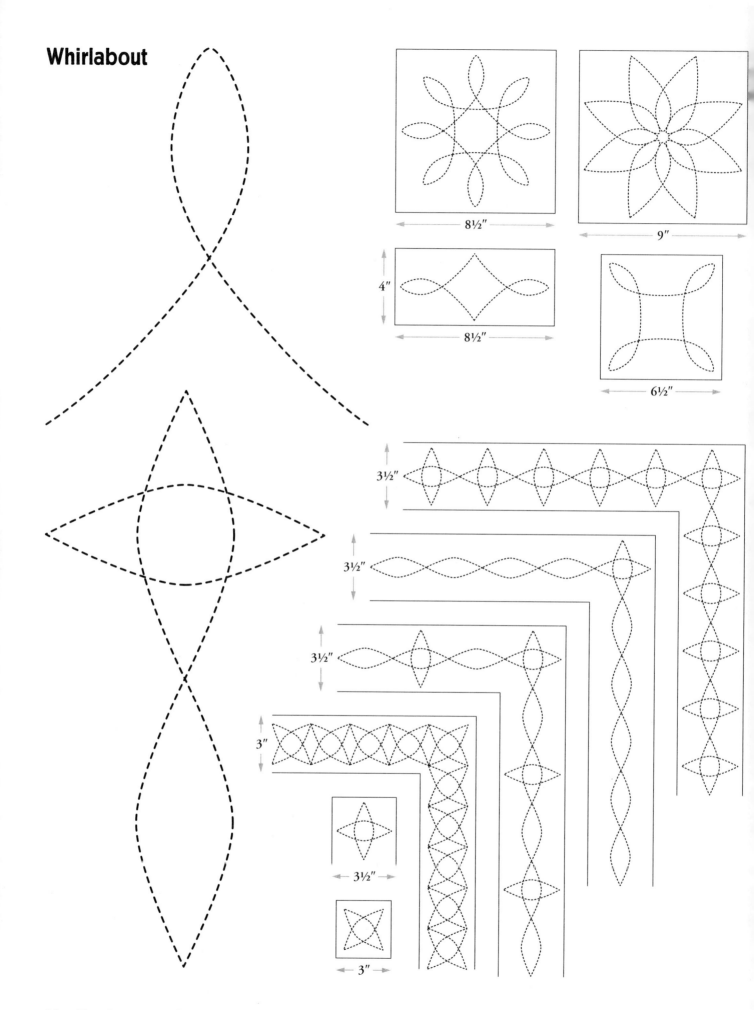

14 ■ The *Quiltmaker* Collection ■ *Quilting Motifs*

Wild Rose

First Bloom

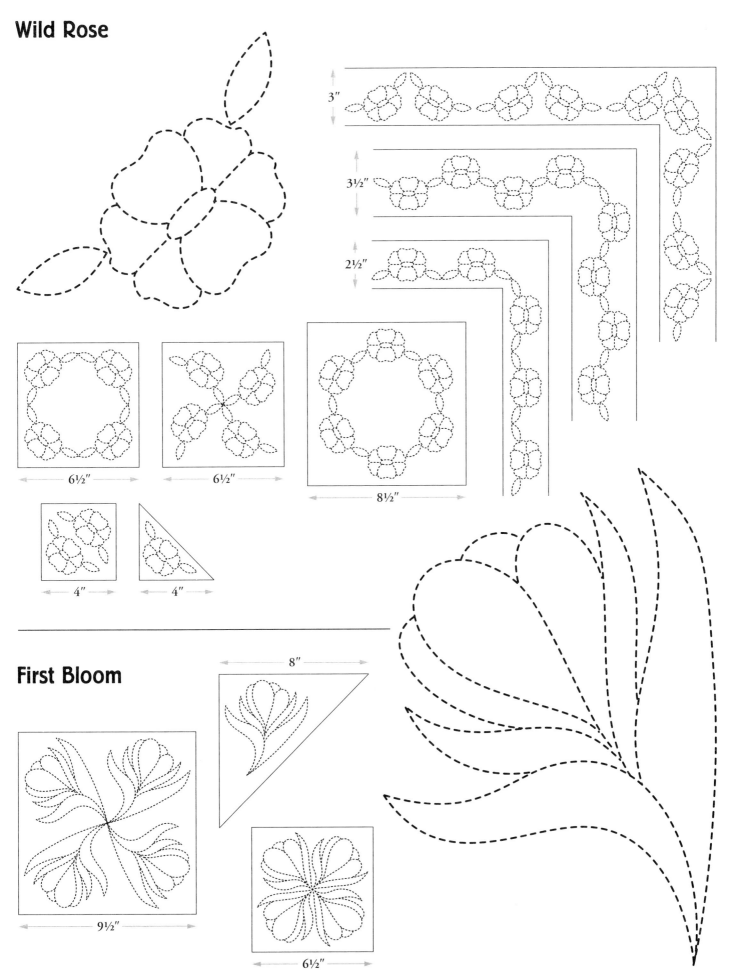

THE *Quiltmaker* COLLECTION ▪ *Quilting Motifs* ▪ 15

Strawberry Fields

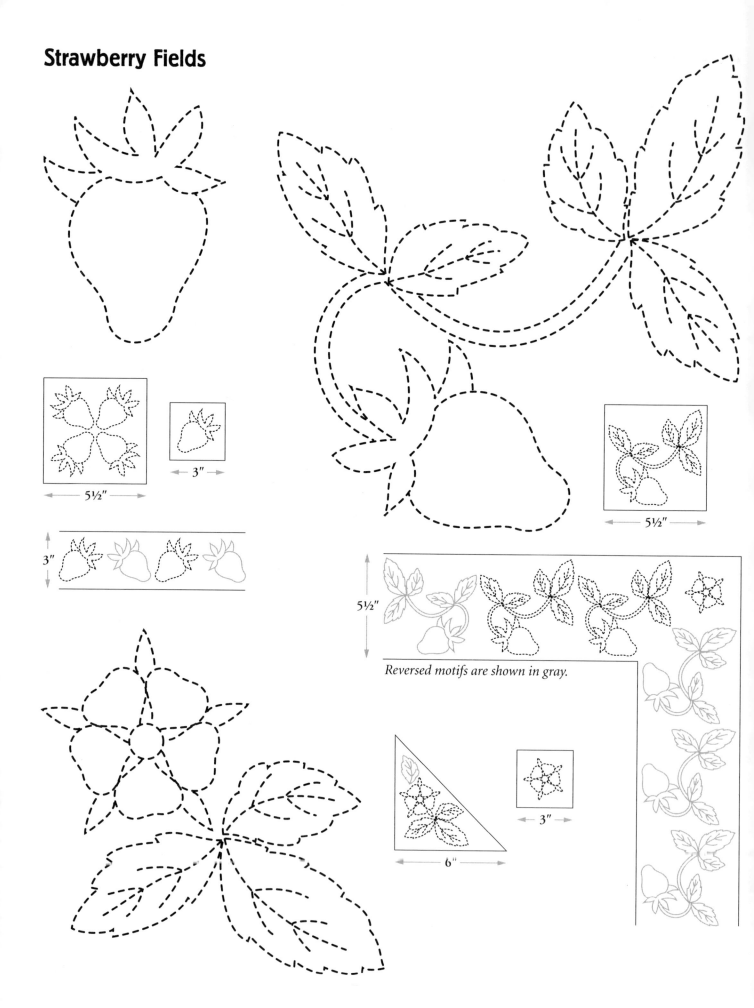

Reversed motifs are shown in gray.

Avalon

In order to make the border motif twine around itself, keep the motif right side up as you mark.

Yes   No

Festive Touch

Festive Touch

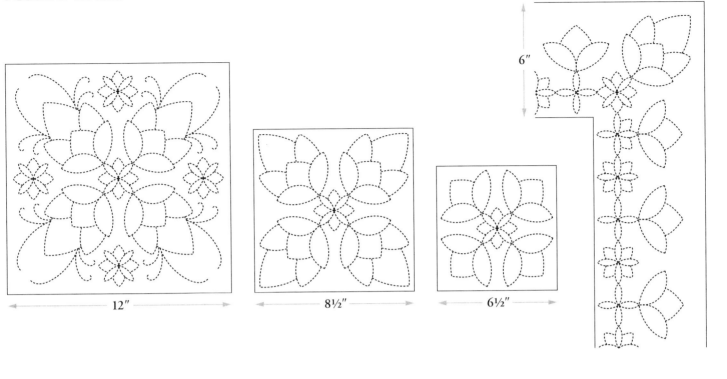

Summer Leaves

Combine Breezy Blossom, page 47, with Summer Leaves.

Thunderbird

For this motif, repeat the zigzag line from the Thunderbird's chest.

Shasta Daisy

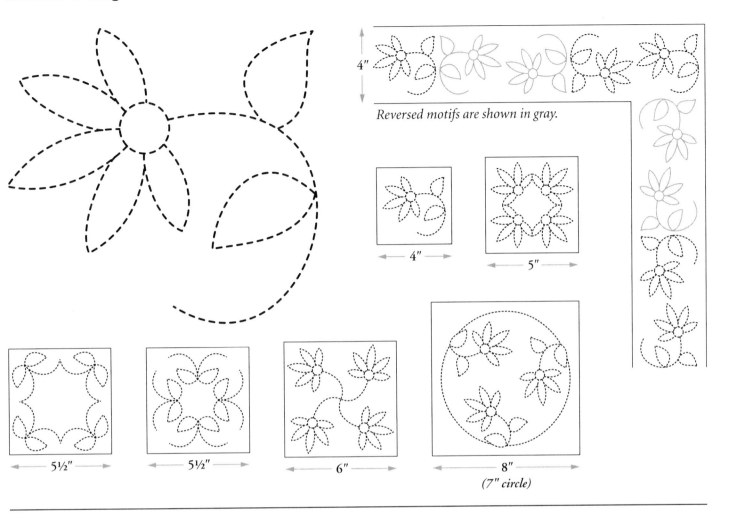

Petite Daisy

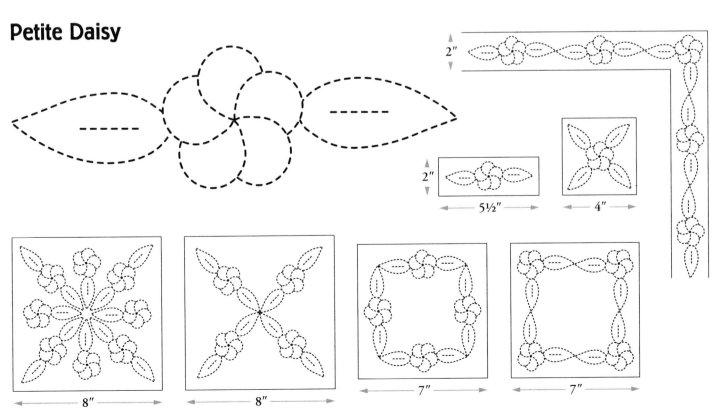

THE QUILTMAKER COLLECTION ■ *Quilting Motifs* ■ 21

Friendship Blossoms

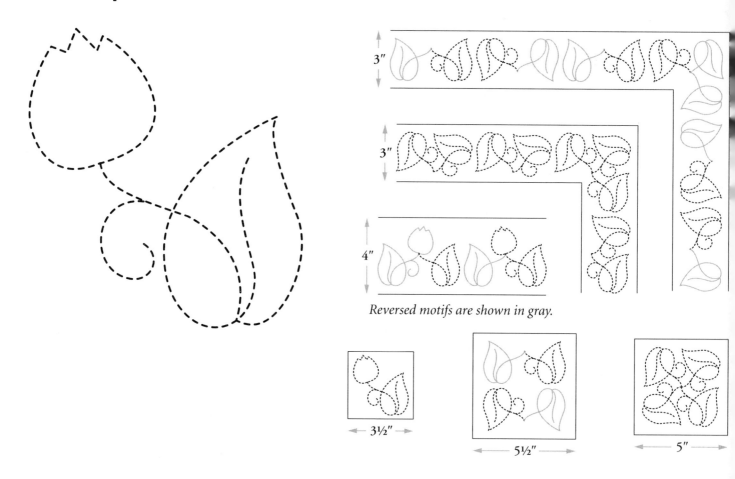

Reversed motifs are shown in gray.

Bell Blossom

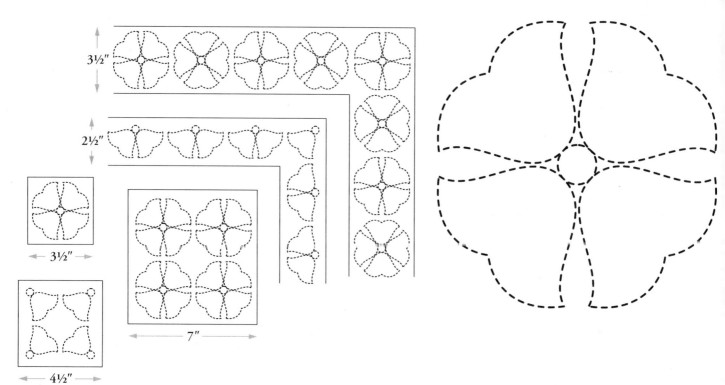

22 ■ THE QUILTMAKER COLLECTION ■ Quilting Motifs

Feathered Wreath

Coleus Leaf

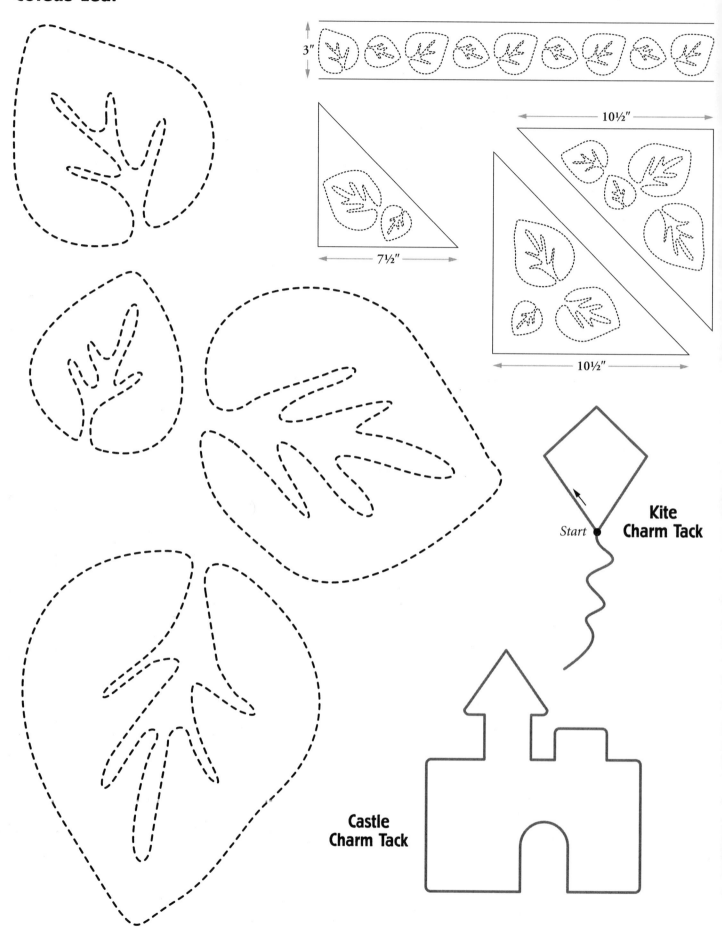

24 ■ THE QUILTMAKER COLLECTION ■ Quilting Motifs

Leaf Cable

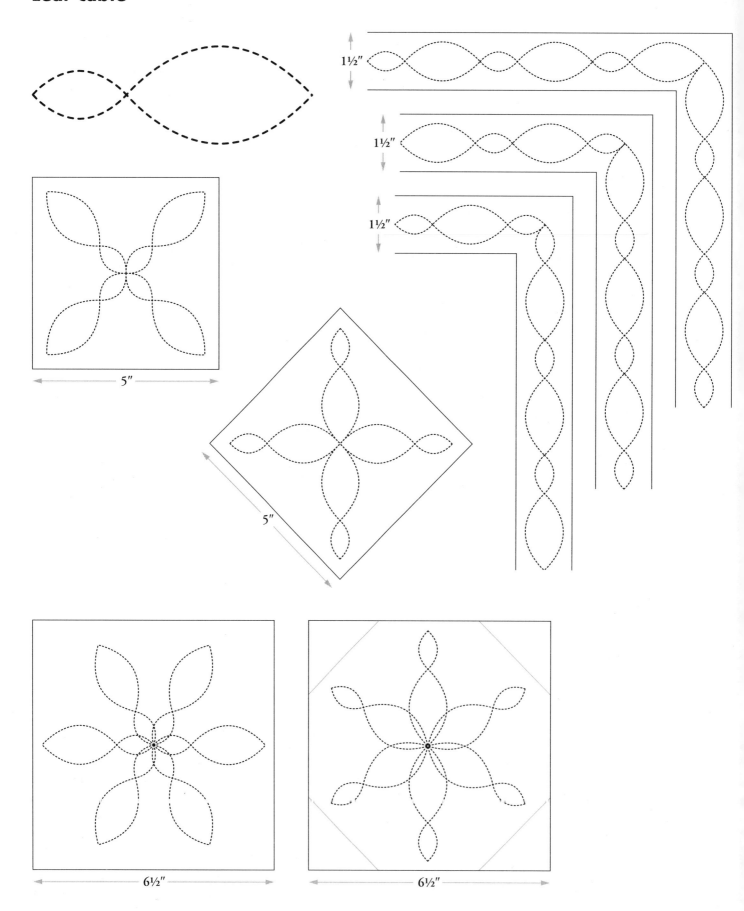

26 ■ The *Quiltmaker* Collection ■ *Quilting Motifs*

Corona

Reversed motifs are shown in gray.

Leaf Trail

Combine Breezy Blossom, page 47, or Bell Blossom, page 22, with the motif above.

Reversed motifs are shown in gray.

Sundae Surprise

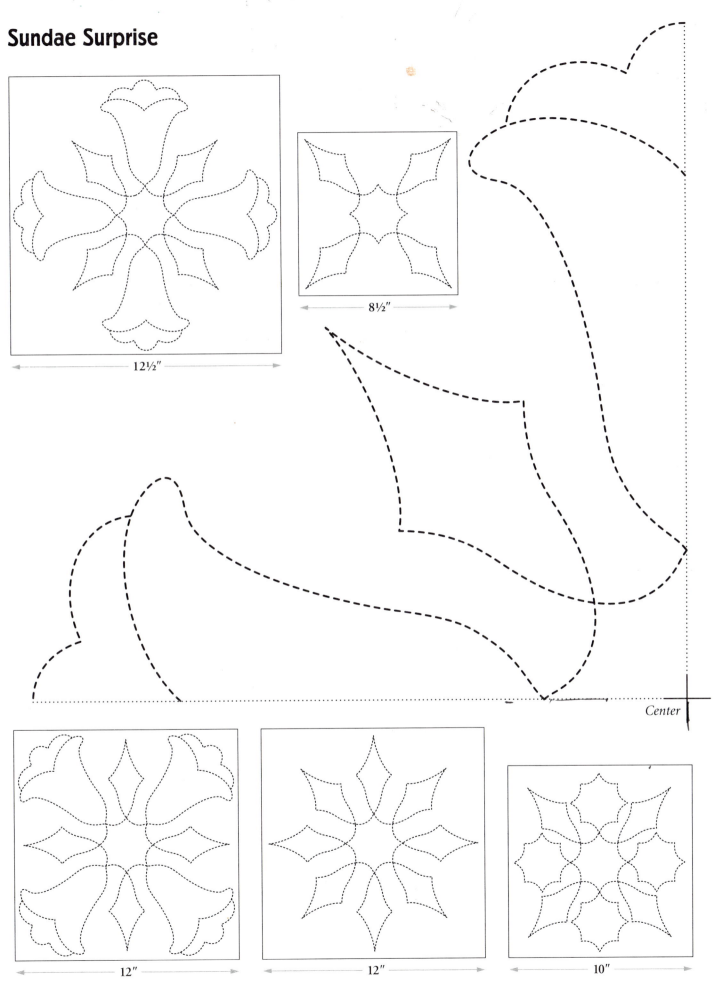

Gift Wrap

5"

9½"

8½"

6½"

12"

30 ■ THE *QUILTMAKER* COLLECTION ■ *Quilting Motifs*

Gift Wrap

Snowflake Charm Tack

5"

5"

6"

Reindeer Charm Tack

THE *QUILTMAKER* COLLECTION ■ *Quilting Motifs* ■ **31**

Star Bound

Reversed motifs are shown in gray.

Twins Charm Tack

Zinnia

Amish Traditions

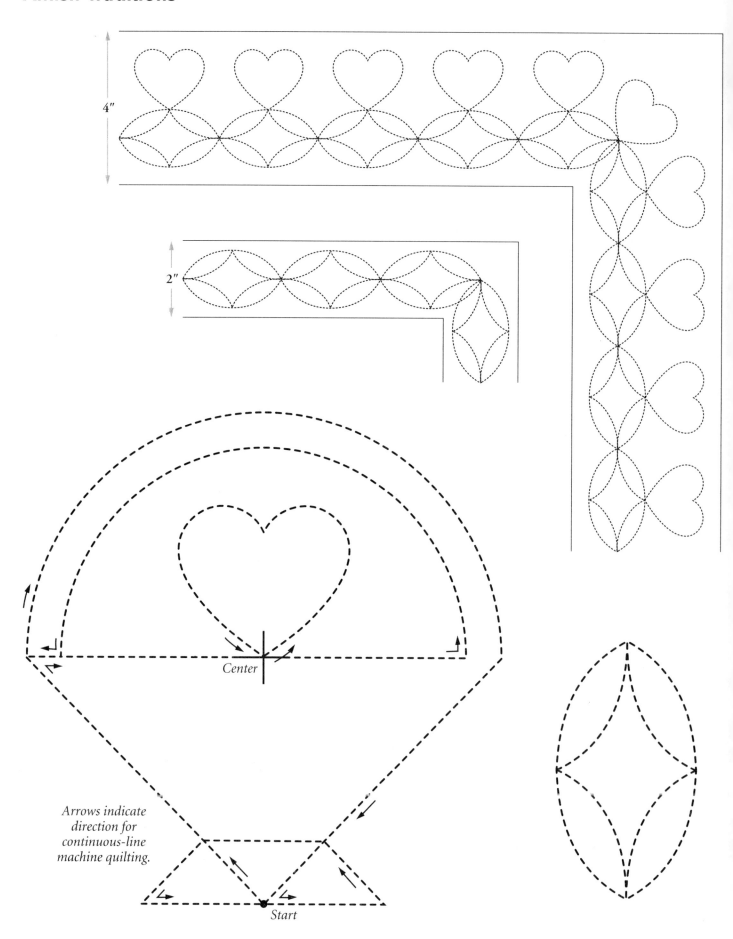

Arrows indicate direction for continuous-line machine quilting.

34 ■ THE QUILTMAKER COLLECTION ■ Quilting Motifs

Amish Traditions

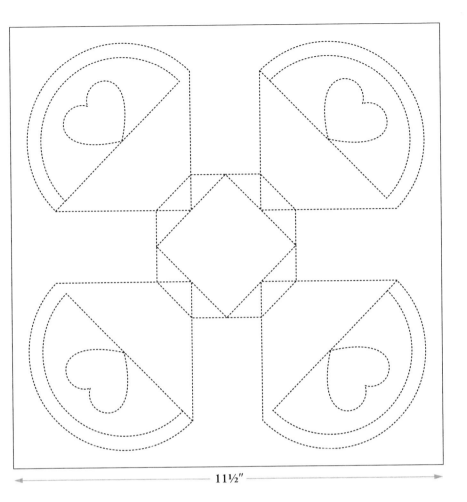
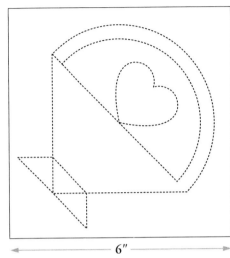

Palace Steps

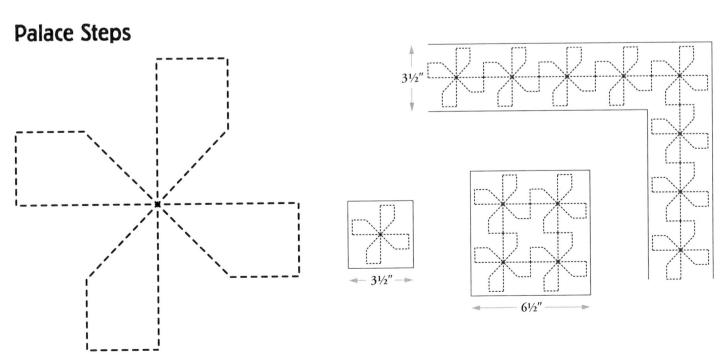

Chinook

Reversed motifs are shown in gray.

Camellia

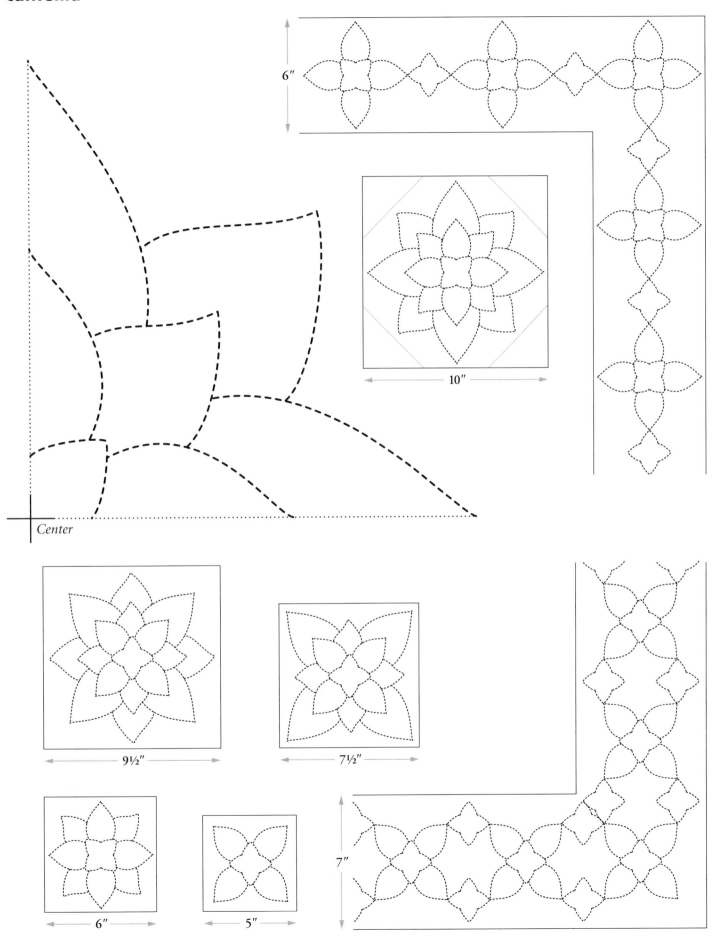

Fanciful Star

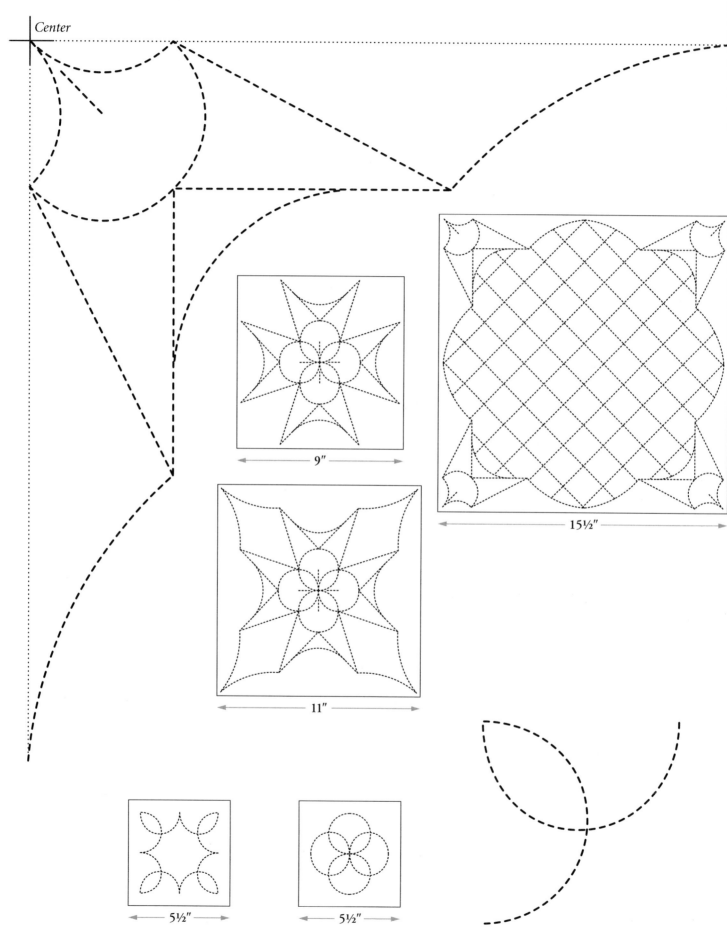

38 ■ THE QUILTMAKER COLLECTION ■ Quilting Motifs

Brocade

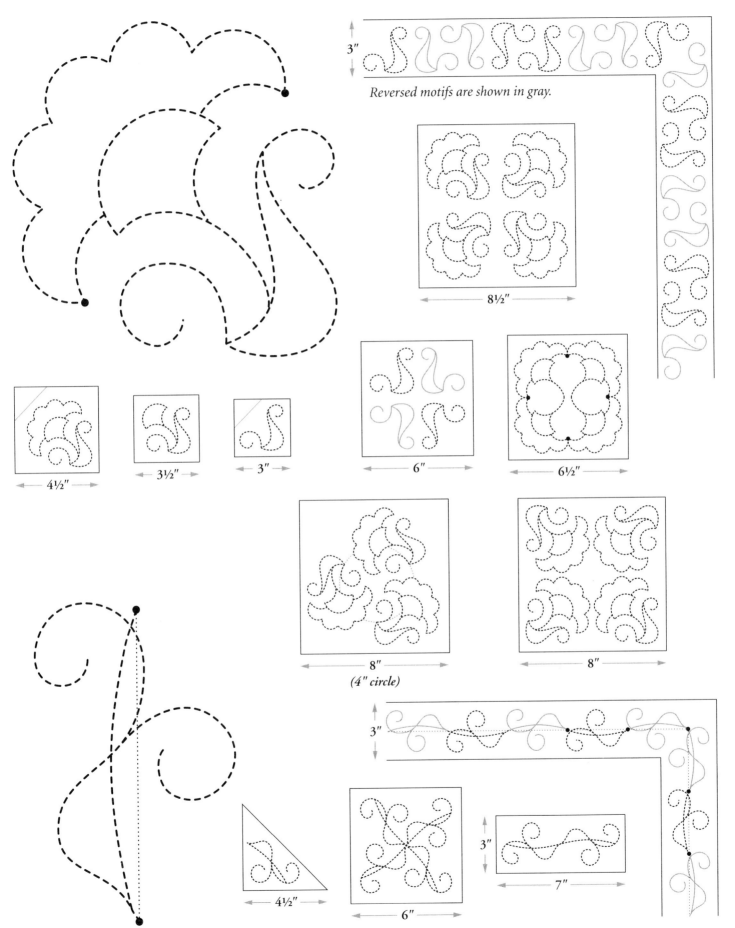

Reversed motifs are shown in gray.

Mariner's Star

Mariner's Star

Apple Tree Charm Tack

Lemon Twist

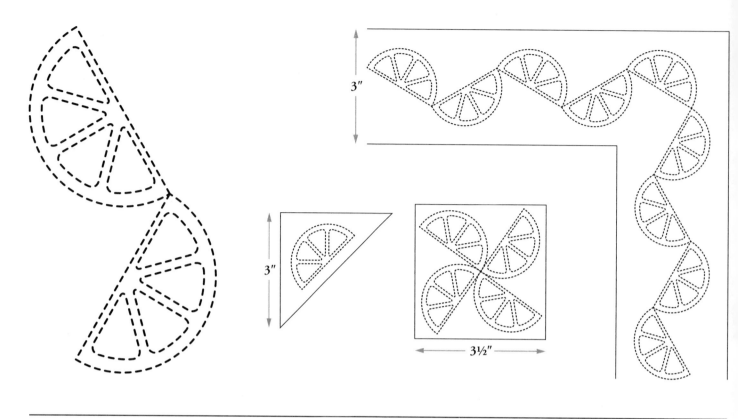

Catch of the Day

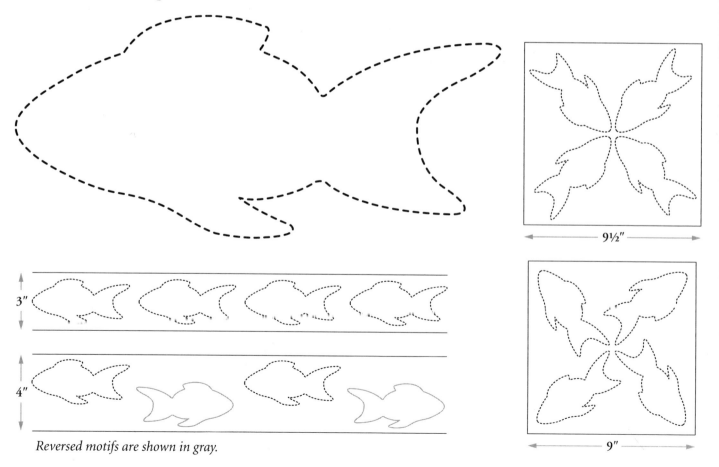

Reversed motifs are shown in gray.

Spring Promise

Reversed motifs are shown in gray.

Feathers & Flowers

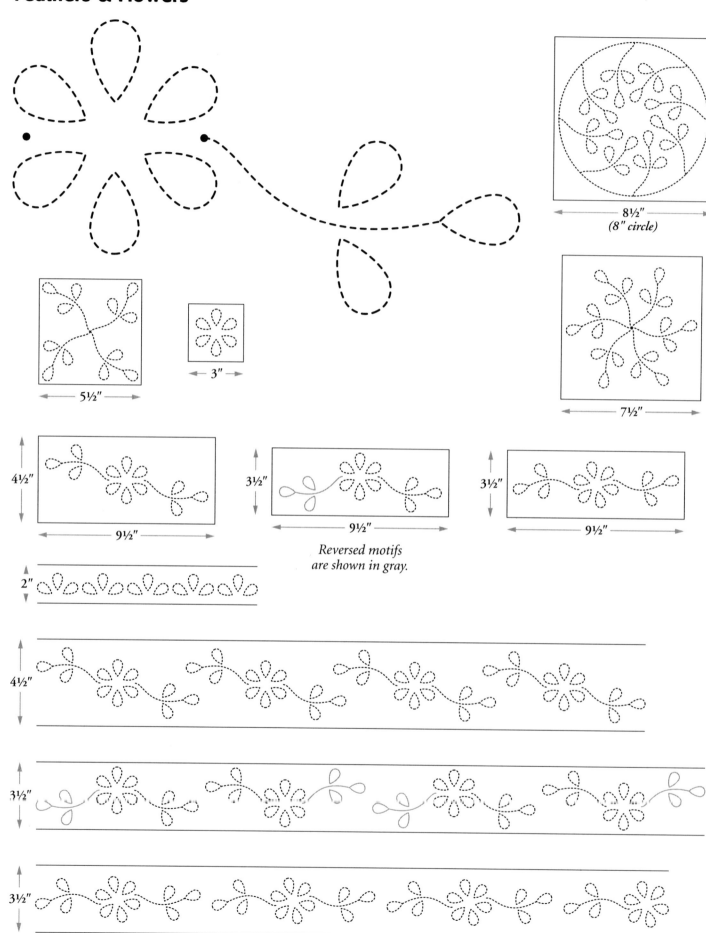

44 ■ THE QUILTMAKER COLLECTION ■ Quilting Motifs

Floating Clouds & Stars

Sunshine

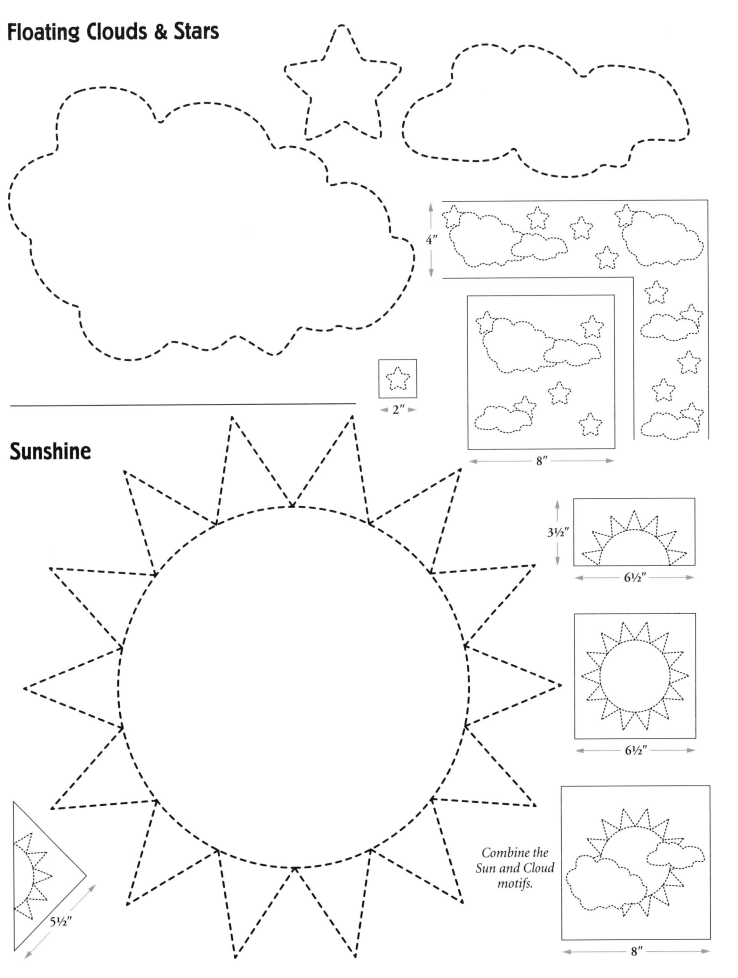

Combine the Sun and Cloud motifs.

Ring of Stars

Breezy Blossom

Crystal Star

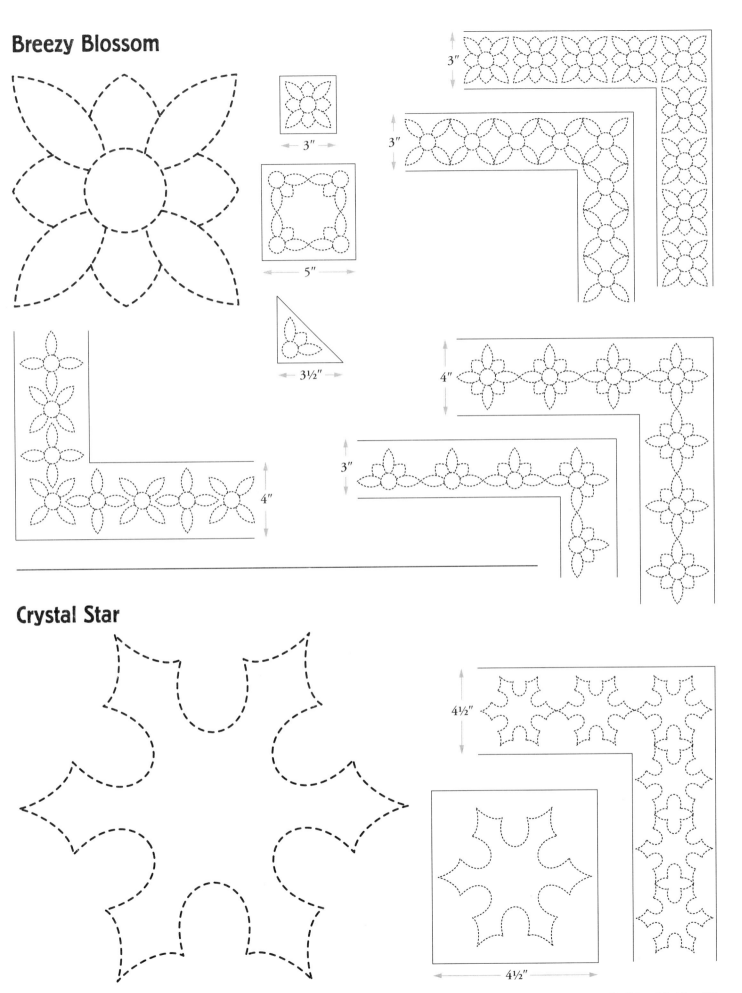

Hearts in Bloom

Hearts in Bloom

For single heart shape, trace the heart that forms the flower.

Butterflies

Scotch Thistle

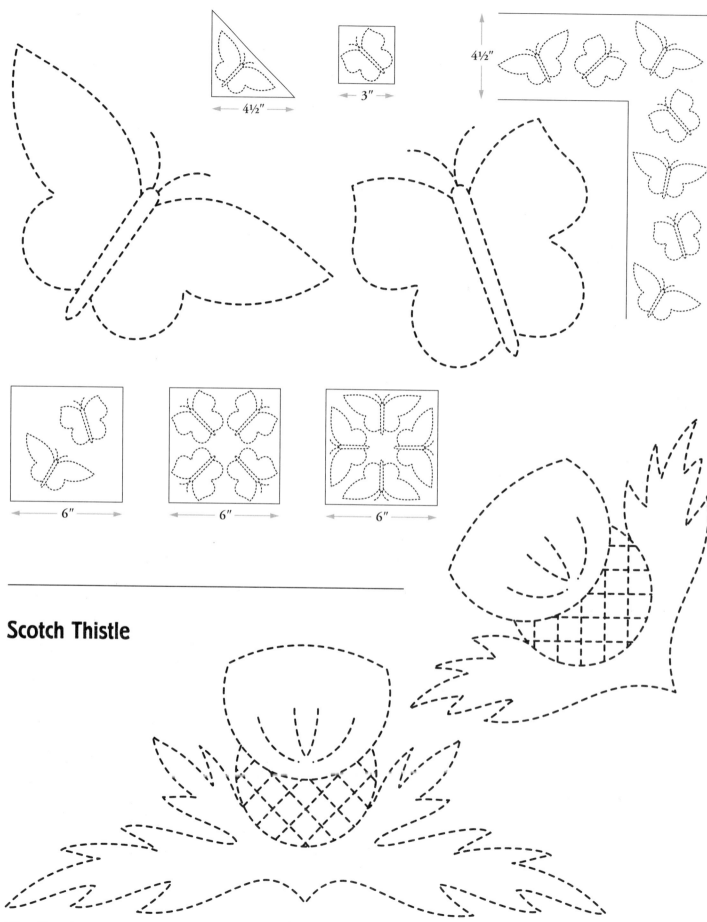

Scotch Thistle

White Dove

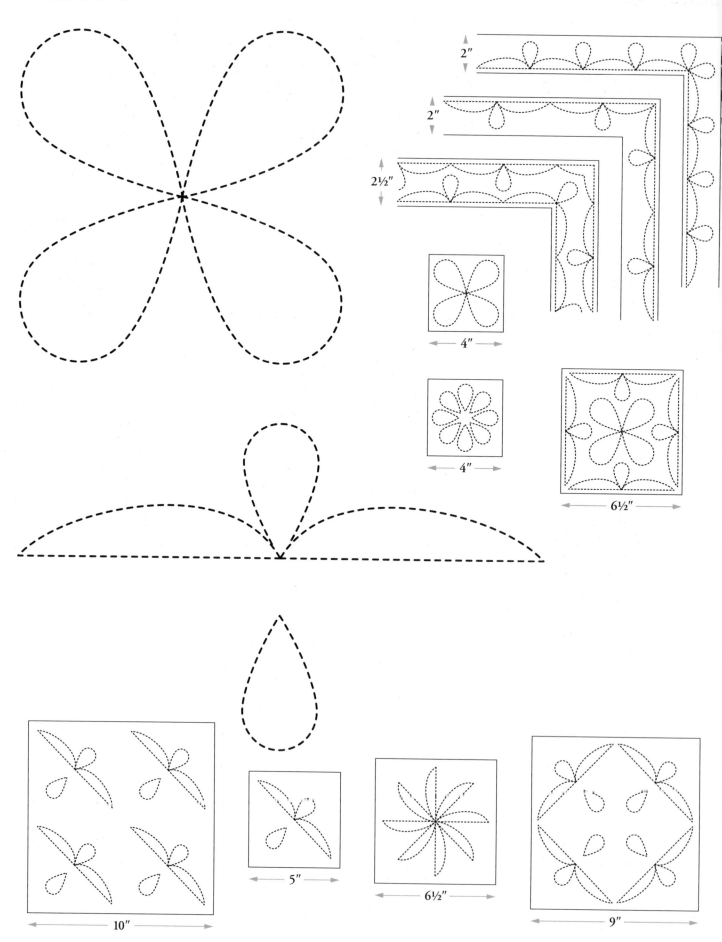

52 ■ THE QUILTMAKER COLLECTION ■ *Quilting Motifs*

Lacy Lock

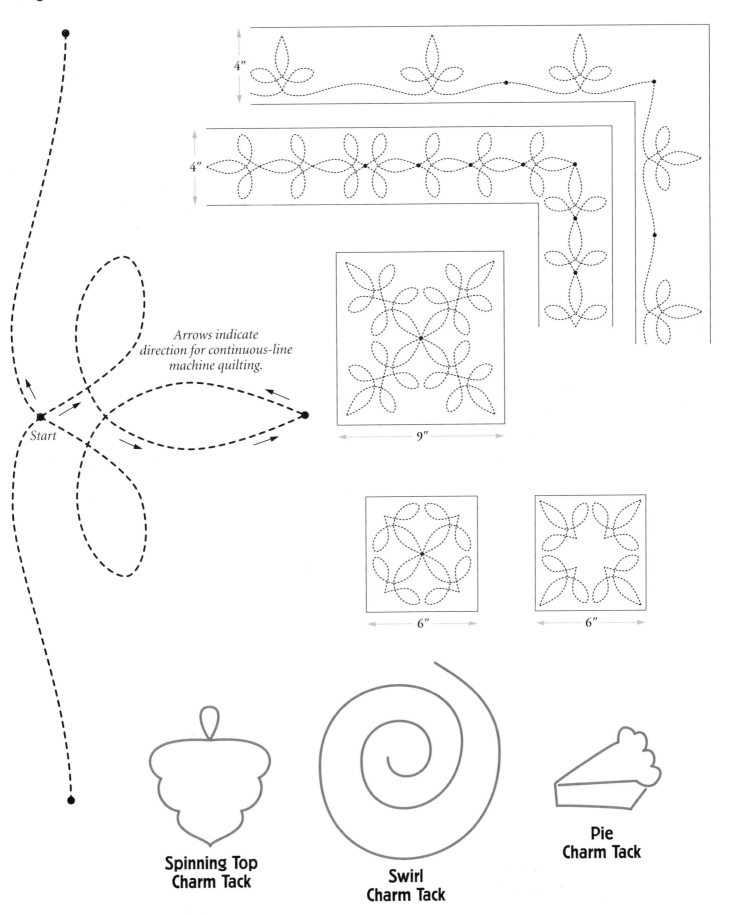

Arrows indicate direction for continuous-line machine quilting.

Spinning Top Charm Tack

Swirl Charm Tack

Pie Charm Tack

Irish Cable

Rabbit Charm Tack

Turtle Charm Tack

Floating Lily

Love's Bloom

Love's Bloom

Cupid's Arrow

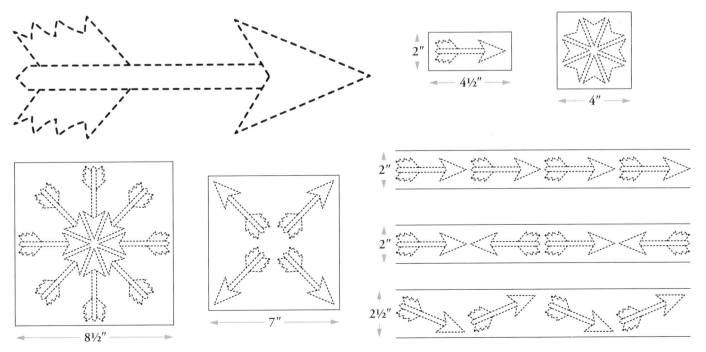

THE *QUILTMAKER* COLLECTION ■ *Quilting Motifs* ■ 57

Fond Memories

58 ▪ THE QUILTMAKER COLLECTION ▪ Quilting Motifs

Twirlaway

Reversed motifs are shown in gray.

These variations use a partial element from the larger Twirlaway motif.

Feather Spray

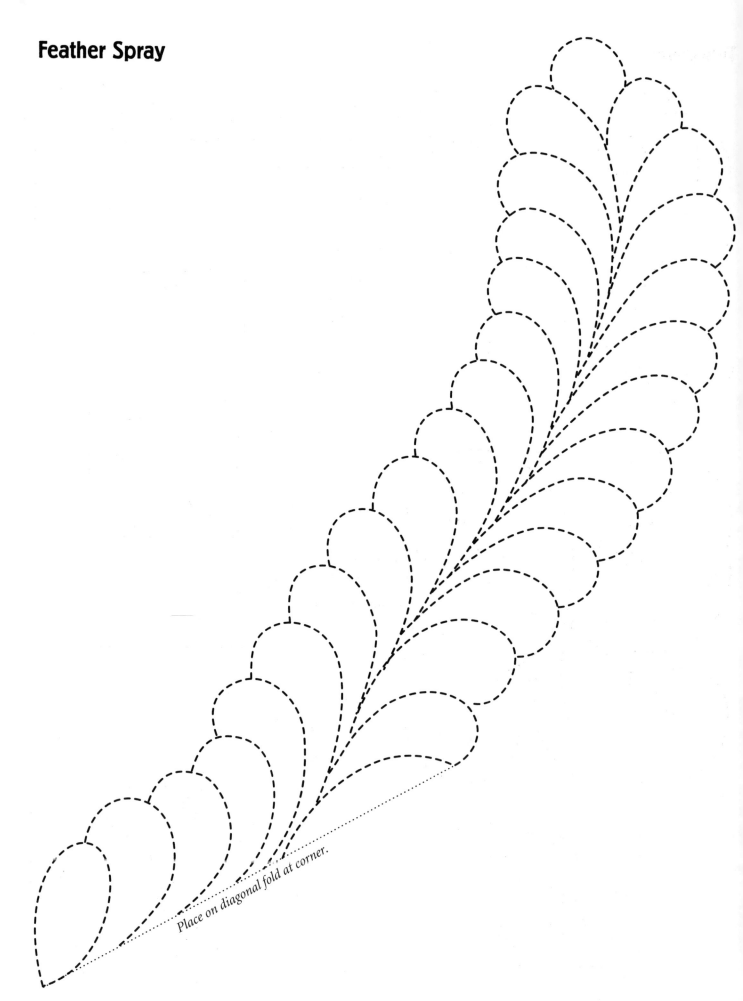

Feather Spray

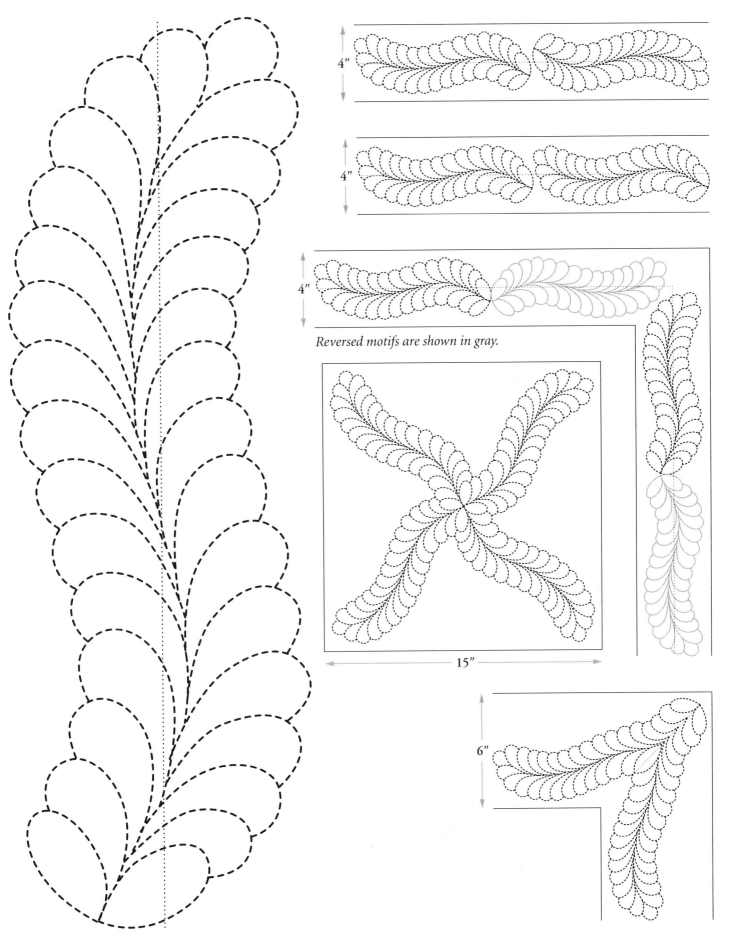

Reversed motifs are shown in gray.

Windswept

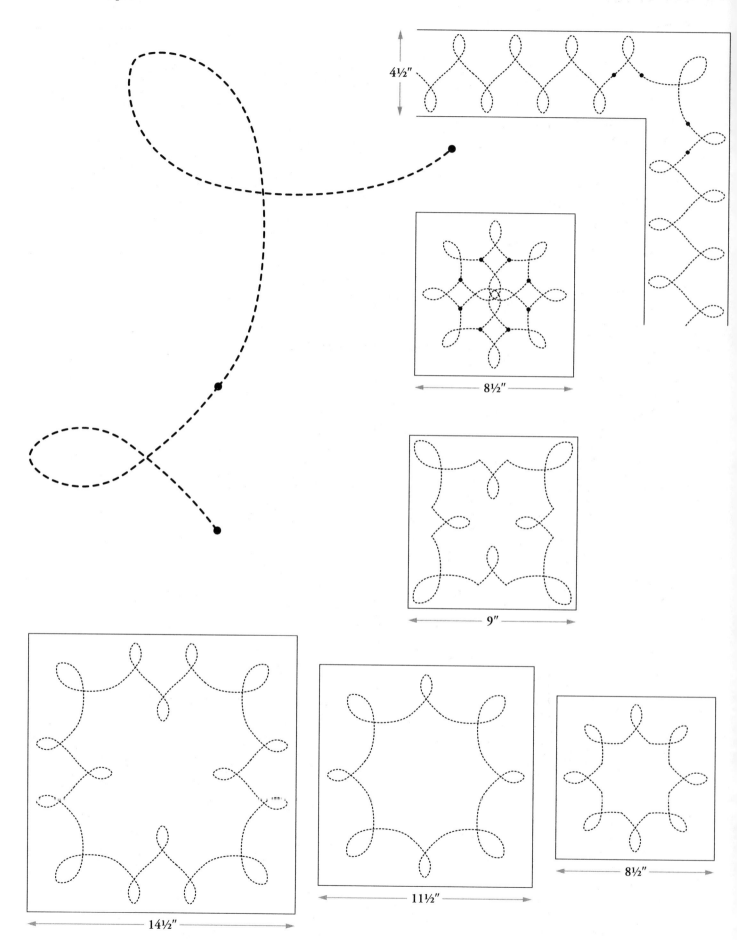

62 ■ THE QUILTMAKER COLLECTION ■ Quilting Motifs

Furrow Cable

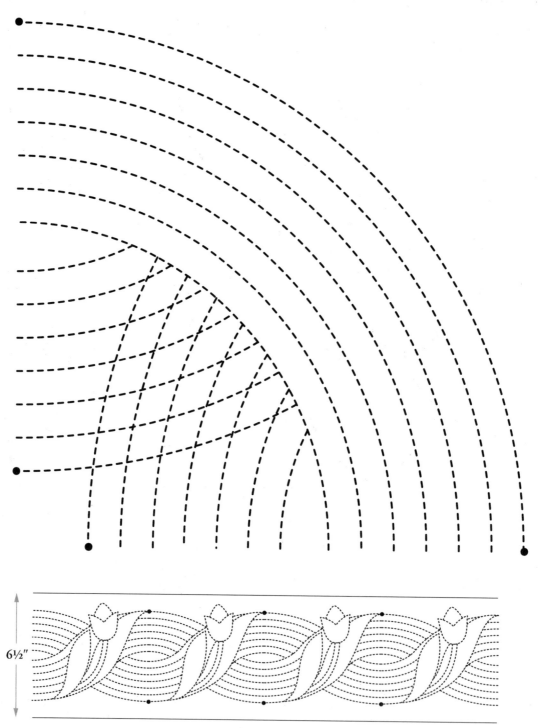

Combine Tulip, page 13, or Flower of Youth, page 63, with Furrow Cable.

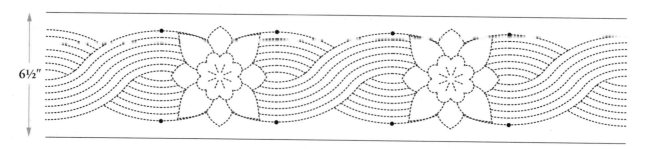

Furrow Cable

6½"

6½"

THE *QUILTMAKER* COLLECTION ▪ *Quilting Motifs* ▪ **65**

April Love

Combine Cupid's Arrow, page 57, with the small heart from April Love.

66 ■ THE QUILTMAKER COLLECTION ■ Quilting Motifs

Ivy

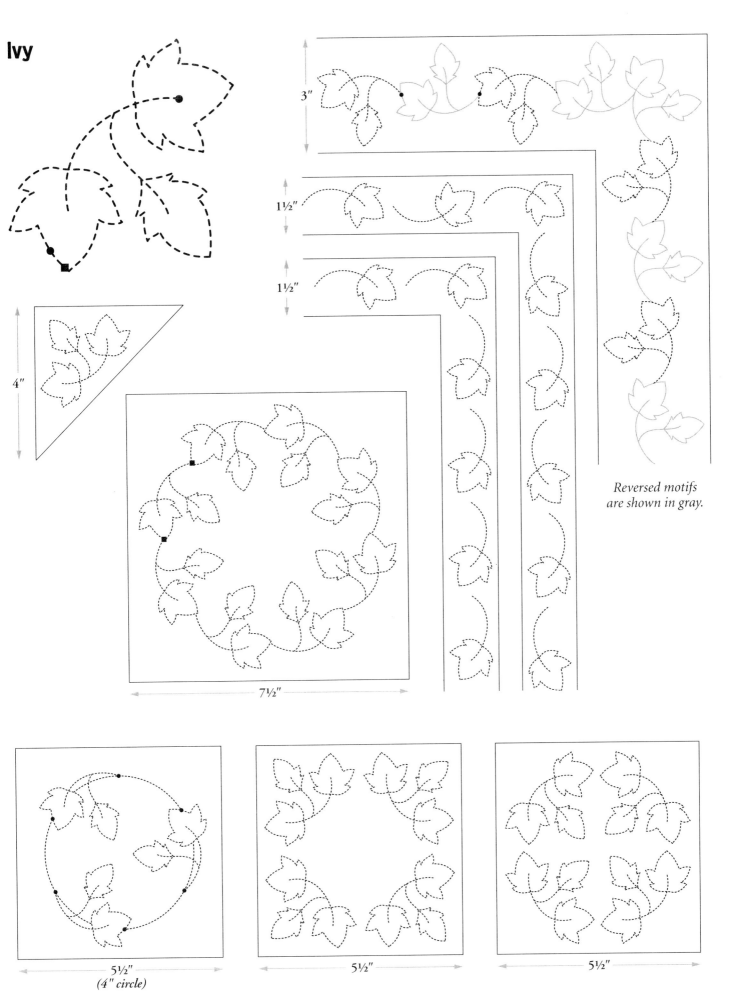

Reversed motifs are shown in gray.

Coventry

68 ■ THE *QUILTMAKER* COLLECTION ■ *Quilting Motifs*

Coventry

Soaring Bird

70 ■ THE QUILTMAKER COLLECTION ■ Quilting Motifs

Hedgerow

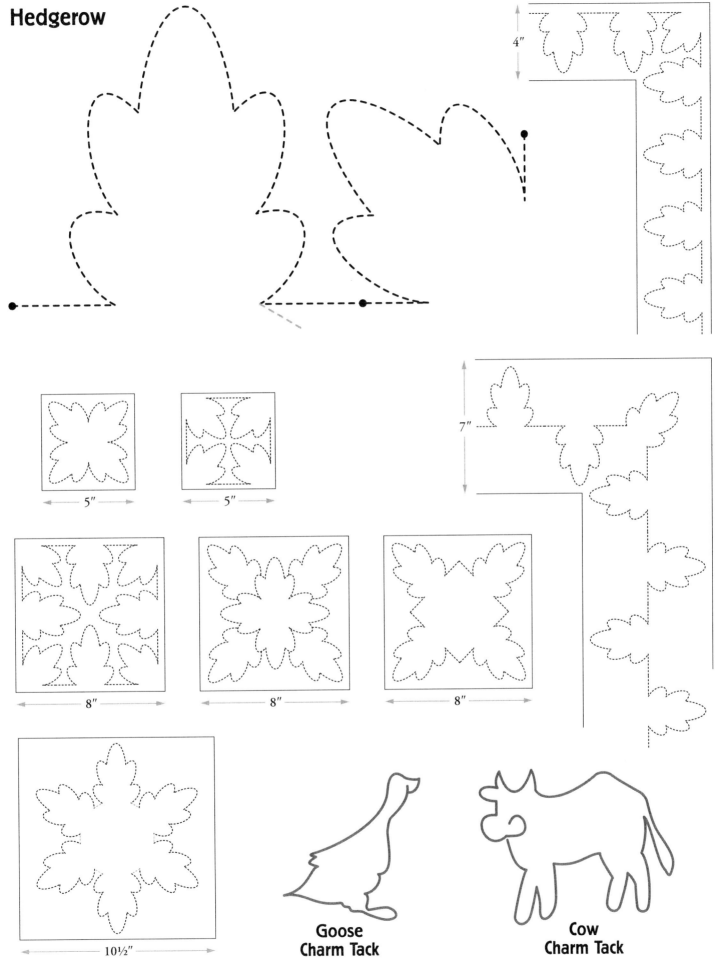

Goose Charm Tack

Cow Charm Tack

Cloverleaf

Double Feather Wreath

Butterfly Garden

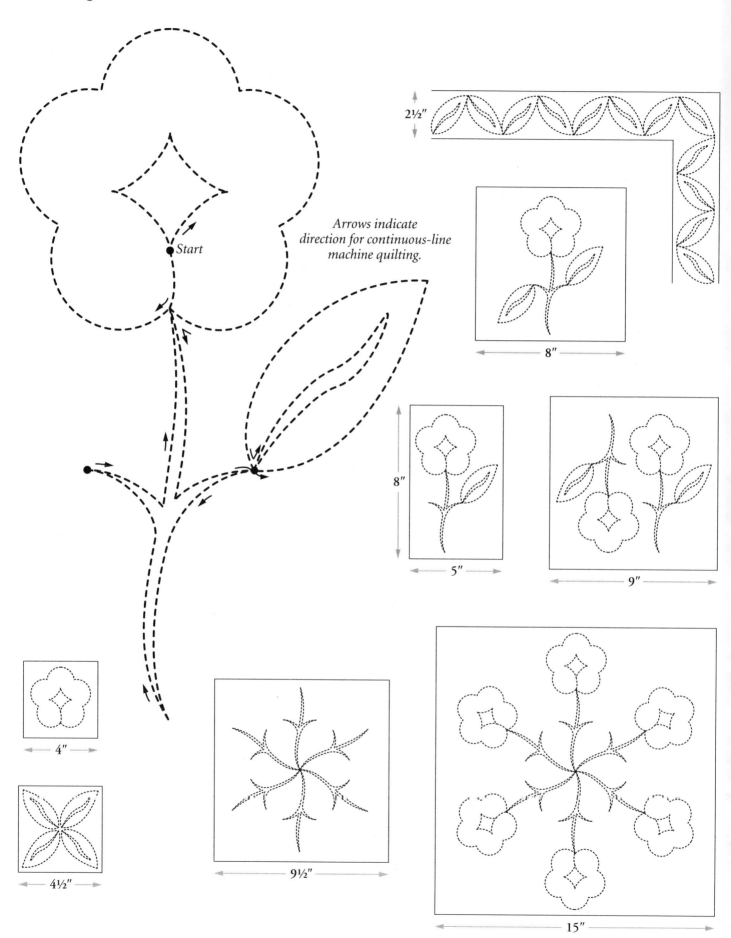

Arrows indicate direction for continuous-line machine quilting.

74 ■ The *Quiltmaker* Collection ■ *Quilting Motifs*

Lotus Bud

Milky Way

Poinsettia

Bunting & Bows

The ribbon from Poinsettia, page 76, can be combined with the bow.

Monarch

Peach Harvest

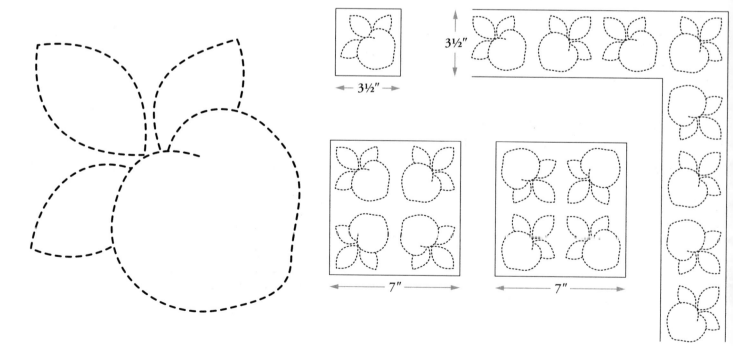

78 ■ The Quiltmaker Collection ■ Quilting Motifs

Rosebush

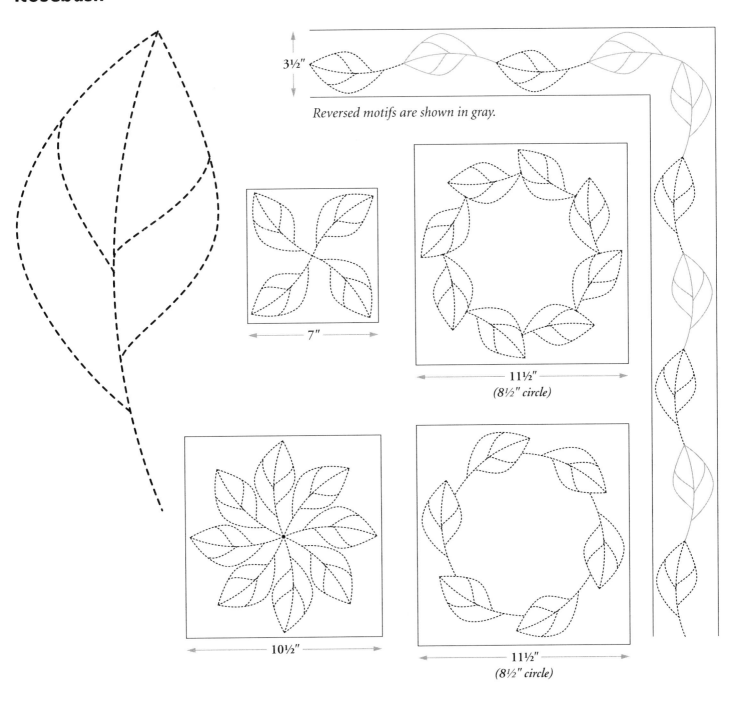

Reversed motifs are shown in gray.

Whirlwind

THE *Quiltmaker* Collection ■ *Quilting Motifs* ■ **79**

Autumn Breeze

Reversed motifs are shown in gray.

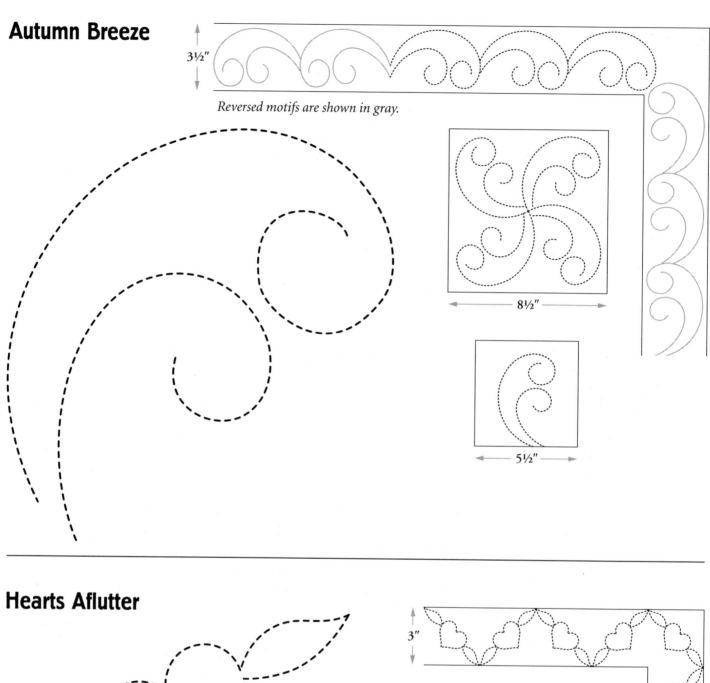

Hearts Aflutter

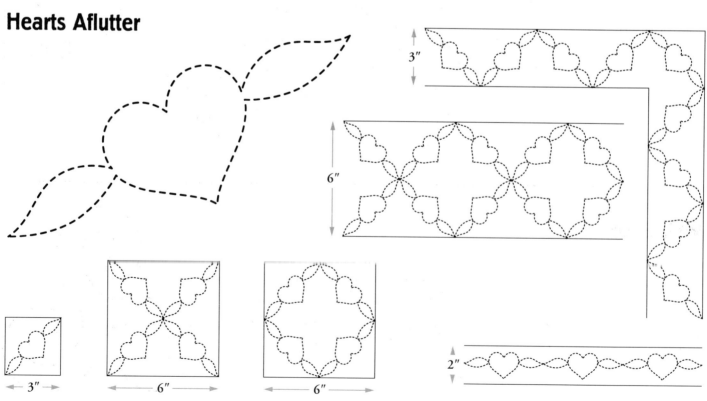

Continuous Cable

Ribbon Reel

Reversed motifs are shown in gray.

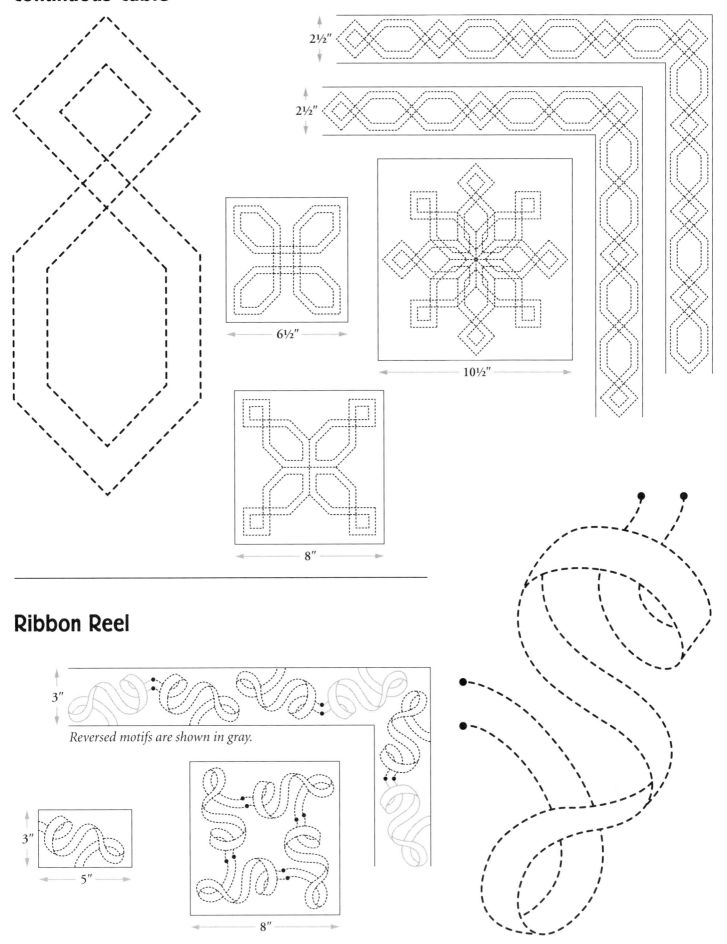

Cover Quilt Pattern

If you just can't wait to try out some of the motifs in this book and you don't have a current project to use them on, how about making your own version of the quilt shown on the cover? You can create one just like ours, or you can substitute other motifs that caught your eye. The quilt goes together so easily that you'll be quilting in no time!

Easy

QUILT SIZE: Wall Quilt 21"x 21"

YARDAGE: (44" fabric)

Dark Peach Print	4" x 4" scrap 1 A
Light Green Print	10"x 15" scrap 4 B
Cream Print	15"x 15" scrap 4 C
Light Blue Print	¼ yard
border strips* sides	2 at 3½"x 15½"
top/bottom	2 at 3½"x 21½"
Dark Blue Print	¼ yard
double-fold binding	3 at 2¼"x 35"
Lining	¾ yard
panel	1 at 25"x 25"
Sleeve	⅓ yard
strip	1 at 9"x 21"
Batting	25"x 25"

SUPPLIES: Various colors of rayon thread.
* Seam allowance is included in the length but no extra has been added for insurance.

Quilting

If you'd like to use different motifs, look in the Size Index under the 6"-block category. Each of these motifs will fit into a cream square. For the border, refer to the 3"-border category.

Referring to the quilting diagram, trace the motifs on each patch. If you plan to use tracing paper for marking, trace motifs on paper.

Layer the lining, batting and quilt top and baste the layers together.

Quilt in the ditch around the center square and each cream square. Quilt each motif. Our cover quilt was machine-quilted using monofilament in the ditch and a different color of rayon thread for each motif.

Finishing

Enclose the edges with binding. Add a sleeve to the back of the quilt so you can hang and enjoy!

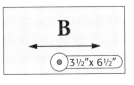
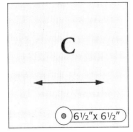

Align arrows with lengthwise or crosswise grain of fabric.

Making the Quilt Top

Referring to the assembly diagram, piece the quilt top. Press seams toward the darker fabrics.

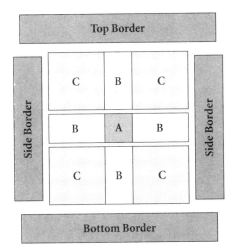

Quilt Assembly

Quilting Motif Placement

Index

Size Index

Squares

2"
Floating Clouds & Stars, 45

2½"
Festive Touch, 18
Garden Party, 25
Mariner's Star, 40
Spring Promise, 43
Star Bound, 32
Whirlwind, 79

3"
Breezy Blossom, 47
Brocade, 39
Butterflies, 50
Corona, 27
Coventry, 69
Double Feather Wreath, 73
Feathers & Flowers, 44
Flower of Youth, 63
Garden Party, 25
Hearts Aflutter, 80
Milky Way, 75
Strawberry Fields, 16
Whirlabout, 14

3½"
April Love, 66
Bell Blossom, 22
Brocade, 39
Cloverleaf, 72
Coventry, 69
Feathered Wreath, 23
Festive Touch, 18
Friendship Blossoms, 22
Leaf Trail, 28
Lemon Twist, 42
Palace Steps, 35
Peach Harvest, 78
Spring Promise, 43
Whirlabout, 14
Zinnia, 33

4"
Avalon, 17
Bunting & Bows, 77
Butterfly Garden, 74
Cloverleaf, 72
Coventry, 69
Cupid's Arrow, 57
Feathered Wreath, 23
Floating Lily, 55
Garden Party, 25
Petite Daisy, 21
Scotch Thistle, 51
Shasta Daisy, 21
Twirlaway, 59
White Dove, 52
Wild Rose, 15

4½"
Bell Blossom, 22
Brocade, 39
Butterfly Garden, 74
Chinook, 36
Cloverleaf, 72
Crystal Star, 47
Festive Touch, 18
Garden Party, 25
Hearts in Bloom, 49
Irish Cable, 54
Lantern Lily, 12
Lida Rose, 10
Lotus Bud, 75
Mariner's Star, 40

5"
Breezy Blossom, 47
Camellia, 37
Corona, 27
Coventry, 69
Friendship Blossoms, 22
Gift Wrap, 30
Hedgerow, 71
Lantern Lily, 12
Leaf Cable, 26
Mariner's Star, 40
Poinsettia, 76
Scotch Thistle, 51
Shasta Daisy, 21
Summer Leaves, 19
White Dove, 52

5½"
April Love, 66
Autumn Breeze, 80
Fanciful Star, 38
Feathered Wreath, 23
Feathers & Flowers, 44
Floating Lily, 55
Friendship Blossoms, 22
Ivy, 67
Shasta Daisy, 21
Star Bound, 32
Strawberry Fields, 16
Thunderbird, 20
Twirlaway, 59
Zinnia, 33

6"
Amish Traditions, 35
Brocade, 39
Butterflies, 50
Camellia, 37
Corona, 27
Coventry, 69
Double Feather Wreath, 73
Festive Touch, 18
Flower of Youth, 63
Hearts Aflutter, 80
Hearts in Bloom, 49
Lacy Lock, 53
Leaf Trail, 28
Lotus Bud, 75

Love's Bloom, 56
Mariner's Star, 40
Monarch, 78
Scotch Thistle, 51
Shasta Daisy, 21

6½"
April Love, 66
Brocade, 39
Continuous Cable, 81
Coventry, 69
Festive Touch, 19
First Bloom, 15
Floating Lily, 55
Lady Luck, 11
Leaf Cable, 26
Leaf Trail, 28
Palace Steps, 35
Ring of Stars, 46
Soaring Bird, 70
Summer Leaves, 19
Sunshine, 45
Whirlabout, 14
White Dove, 52
Wild Rose, 15

7"
April Love, 66
Bell Blossom, 22
Corona, 27
Cupid's Arrow, 57
Feathered Wreath, 23
Leaf Trail, 28
Peach Harvest, 78
Petite Daisy, 21
Rosebush, 79
Scotch Thistle, 51

7½"
Camellia, 37
Feathers & Flowers, 44
Ivy, 67
Lotus Bud, 75
Love's Bloom, 56
Mariner's Star, 40
Star Bound, 32
Thunderbird, 20
Tulip, 13
Zinnia, 33

8"
Brocade, 39
Bunting & Bows, 77
Butterfly Garden, 74
Continuous Cable, 81
Floating Clouds & Stars, 45
Flower of Youth, 63
Hearts in Bloom, 49
Hedgerow, 71
Irish Cable, 54
Leaf Trail, 28
Lida Rose, 10
Love's Bloom, 56
Petite Daisy, 21
Ribbon Reel, 81

Shasta Daisy, 21
Soaring Bird, 70
Sunshine, 45
Zinnia, 33

8½"
Autumn Breeze, 80
Brocade, 39
Chinook, 36
Cupid's Arrow, 57
Feathers & Flowers, 44
Festive Touch, 19
Floating Lily, 55
Gift Wrap, 30
Hearts in Bloom, 48–49
Sundae Surprise, 29
Twirlaway, 59
Whirlabout, 14
Wild Rose, 15
Windswept, 62

9"
Bunting & Bows, 77
Butterfly Garden, 74
Catch of the Day, 42
Fanciful Star, 38
Garden Party, 25
Hearts in Bloom, 48
Lacy Lock, 53
Lida Rose, 10
Summer Leaves, 19
Whirlabout, 14
White Dove, 52
Windswept, 62

9½"
Butterfly Garden, 74
Camellia, 37
Catch of the Day, 42
Chinook, 36
First Bloom, 15
Flower of Youth, 63
Mariner's Star, 40

10"
April Love, 66
Camellia, 37
Chinook, 36
Floating Lily, 55
Fond Memories, 58
Sundae Surprise, 29
Tulip, 13
White Dove, 52

10½"
Continuous Cable, 81
Hedgerow, 71
Love's Bloom, 56
Rosebush, 79

11"
Fanciful Star, 38
Floating Lily, 55

11½″
Amish Traditions, 35
Rosebush, 79
Windswept, 62

12″
Feathered Wreath, 23
Festive Touch, 19
Fond Memories, 58
Garden Party, 25
Gift Wrap, 30
Sundae Surprise, 29

12½″
Monarch, 78
Sundae Surprise, 29

13″
Lida Rose, 10
Mariner's Star, 40

14″
Fond Memories, 58

14½″
Windswept, 62

15″
Butterfly Garden, 74
Feather Spray, 61
Garden Party, 25

15½″
Fanciful Star, 38

Rectangles
If you don't find the dimensions you need, match the height of your rectangle with border motifs and see if repeats fit into your rectangle area.

4″ x 2″
Twirlaway, 59

4½″ x 2″
Cupid's Arrow, 57

4½″ x 3½″
Cloverleaf, 72

5″ x 3″
Ribbon Reel, 81

5″ x 3½″
Spring Promise, 43

5½″ x 2″
Petite Daisy, 21

5½″ x 2½″
Lantern Lily, 12

6″ x 3″
Double Feather Wreath, 73
Garden Party, 25

6½″ x 3″
Garden Party, 25

6½″ x 3½″
Sunshine, 45

7″ x 2½″
Double Feather Wreath, 73

7″ x 3″
Brocade, 39
Flower of Youth, 63

7½″ x 2½″
Star Bound, 32

8″ x 5″
Butterfly Garden, 74

8½″ x 4″
Whirlabout, 14

9″ x 4″
Tulip, 13

9″ x 2″
Summer Leaves, 19

9½″ x 3½″
Feathers & Flowers, 44

9½″ x 4½″
Feathers & Flowers, 44
Mariner's Star, 40

11″ x 4″
Lida Rose, 10

12″ x 3″
Coventry, 69

15″ x 3″
Garden Party, 25

17½″ x 4″
Tulip, 13

Triangles
(measured on short side)

3″
Leaf Trail, 28
Lemon Twist, 42

3½″
April Love, 66
Breezy Blossom, 47

4″
Cloverleaf, 72
Floating Lily, 55
Garden Party, 25
Ivy, 67
Wild Rose, 15

4½″
Brocade, 39
Butterflies, 50
Double Feather Wreath, 73
Lotus Bud, 75

5″
Soaring Bird, 70
Star Bound, 32

5½″
Mariner's Star, 40
Sunshine, 45
Zinnia, 33

6″
Double Feather Wreath, 73
Ring of Stars, 46
Scotch Thistle, 51
Strawberry Fields, 16

6½″
April Love, 66
Gift Wrap, 30
Hearts in Bloom, 48–49
Lady Luck, 11
Lida Rose, 10

7″
Coventry, 69

7½″
Coleus Leaf, 24

8″
First Bloom, 15

8½″
Feathered Wreath, 23

9½″
Gift Wrap, 30

10½″
Coleus Leaf, 24

11″
Poinsettia, 76

12″
Feathered Wreath, 23

15″
Poinsettia, 76

Octagons

6″
Corona, 27

6½″
Lady Luck, 11
Leaf Cable, 26

10″
Camellia, 37

10½″
Hearts in Bloom, 48

Circular Designs Within a Square
(dimension reflects square)

5″
Lantern Lily, 12

5½″
Ivy, 67

6″
Corona, 27

6½″
Lady Luck, 11
Ring of Stars, 46

7″
Corona, 27

7½″
Ivy, 67

8″
Shasta Daisy, 21

8½″
Feathers & Flowers, 44
Hearts in Bloom, 48

10″
Tulip, 13

10½″
Love's Bloom, 56

12″
Feathered Wreath, 23
Gift Wrap, 30

13″
Lida Rose, 10

15″
Butterfly Garden, 74

Borders
A motif that fits in a square can also be used for a border. Select one with the same measurement as the border width you wish to fill and repeat the design along the lengths.

1½″
Ivy, 67
Leaf Cable, 26

2″
Amish Traditions, 34
Cloverleaf, 72
Cupid's Arrow, 57
Feathers & Flowers, 44
Hearts Aflutter, 80
Petite Daisy, 21
Spring Promise, 43
Summer Leaves, 19
Thunderbird, 20
Twirlaway, 59
White Dove, 52

2½″
April Love, 66
Bell Blossom, 22
Butterfly Garden, 74
Cloverleaf, 72
Continuous Cable, 81
Cupid's Arrow, 57
Double Feather Wreath, 73

THE *QUILTMAKER* COLLECTION ▪ *Quilting Motifs* ▪ **85**

Borders, continued

(2½")
Leaf Trail, 28
Mariner's Star, 40
Spring Promise, 43
Star Bound, 32
Whirlwind, 79
White Dove, 52
Wild Rose, 15

3"
Avalon, 17
Brocade, 39
Breezy Blossom, 47
Bunting & Bows, 77
Catch of the Day, 42
Cloverleaf, 72
Coleus Leaf, 24
Feathered Wreath, 23
Flower of Youth, 63
Friendship Blossoms, 22
Hearts Aflutter, 80
Ivy, 67
Lemon Twist, 42
Lotus Bud, 75
Ribbon Reel, 81
Soaring Bird, 70
Strawberry Fields, 16
Whirlabout, 14
Wild Rose, 15

3½"
Autumn Breeze, 80
Bell Blossom, 22
Bunting & Bows, 77
Corona, 27
Cloverleaf, 72
Feathered Wreath, 23
Feathers & Flowers, 44
Floating Lily, 55
Hearts in Bloom, 49
Leaf Trail, 28
Palace Steps, 35
Peach Harvest, 78
Ring of Stars, 46
Rosebush, 79
Spring Promise, 43
Whirlabout, 14
Wild Rose, 15
Zinnia, 33

4"
Amish Traditions, 34
April Love, 66
Breezy Blossom, 47
Bunting & Bows, 77
Catch of the Day, 42
Chinook, 36
Feather Spray, 61
Festive Touch, 18
Floating Clouds & Stars, 45
Friendship Blossoms, 22

Hearts in Bloom, 49
Hedgerow, 71
Irish Cable, 54
Lacy Lock, 53
Lantern Lily, 12
Lida Rose, 10
Love's Bloom, 57
Mariner's Star, 41
Shasta Daisy, 21
Tulip, 13

4½"
Butterflies, 50
Cloverleaf, 72
Crystal Star, 47
Feathers & Flowers, 44
Floating Lily, 55
Irish Cable, 54
Lotus Bud, 75
Love's Bloom, 57
Mariner's Star, 41
Scotch Thistle, 51
Soaring Bird, 70
Spring Promise, 43
Windswept, 62
Zinnia, 33

5"
Chinook, 36
Floating Lily, 55
Flower of Youth, 63
Gift Wrap, 30

5½"
Strawberry Fields, 16

6"
Camellia, 37
Feather Spray, 61
Festive Touch, 19
Gift Wrap, 30
Hearts Aflutter, 80

6½"
Furrow Cable, 64–65

7"
Camellia, 37
Flower of Youth, 63
Hedgerow, 71

Subject Index

Aquatic Animals
Catch of the Day, 42
Turtle Charm Tack, 54

Birds
Goose Charm Tack, 71
Soaring Bird, 70
Thunderbird, 20

Butterflies
Butterflies, 50
Butterfly Charm Tack, 25
Monarch, 78

Creatures and People
Butterflies, 50
Butterfly Charm Tack, 25
Catch of the Day, 42
Cow Charm Tack, 71
Goose Charm Tack, 71
Monarch, 78
Rabbit Charm Tack, 54
Soaring Bird, 70
Thunderbird, 20
Turtle Charm Tack, 54
Twins Charm Tack, 32

Feathers
Double Feather Wreath, 73
Feathered Wreath, 23
Feather Spray, 60–61
Monarch, 78

Flowers
Bell Blossom, 22
Breezy Blossom, 47
Brocade, 39
Butterfly Garden, 74
Camellia, 37
Cloverleaf, 72
Corona, 27
Coventry, 69
Feathers & Flowers, 44
Festive Touch, 18
First Bloom, 15
Floating Lily, 55
Flower of Youth, 63
Fond Memories, 58
Friendship Blossoms, 22
Furrow Cable (variations), 64
Garden Party, 25
Hearts in Bloom, 49
Lantern Lily, 12
Lida Rose, 10
Lotus Bud, 75
Love's Bloom, 56
Petite Daisy, 21
Scotch Thistle, 51
Shasta Daisy, 21
Spring Promise, 43
Strawberry Fields, 16
Tulip, 13
White Dove (variations), 52
Wild Rose, 15
Zinnia, 33

Food
Catch of the Day, 42
Lemon Twist, 42
Peach Harvest, 78
Pie Charm Tack, 53
Strawberry Fields, 16
Sundae Surprise, 29

Children's Themes
Apple Tree Charm Tack, 41
Castle Charm Tack, 24

Catch of the Day, 42
Cow Charm Tack, 71
Kite Charm Tack, 24
Rabbit Charm Tack, 54
Spinning Top Charm Tack, 53
Turtle Charm Tack, 54
Twins Charm Tack, 32

Independence Day
Milky Way, 75
Pie Charm Tack, 53
Ring of Stars, 46

Hearts/ Valentine's Day
Amish Traditions, 34
April Love, 66
Bunting & Bows, 77
Cupid's Arrow, 57
Double Heart Charm Tack, 25
Hearts Aflutter, 80
Hearts in Bloom, 49
Love's Bloom, 56
Ribbon Reel, 81

Leaves
(independent from flowers)
Amish Traditions, 34
Butterfly Garden (variations), 74
Cloverleaf, 72
Coleus Leaf, 24
Corona, 27
Feathered Wreath (variations), 23
Feathers & Flowers (variations), 44
Floating Lily (variations), 55
Friendship Blossoms, 22
Garden Party (variations), 25
Hedgerow, 71
Ivy, 67
Leaf Cable, 26
Leaf Trail, 28
Rosebush, 79
Spring Promise (variations), 43
Summer Leaves (variations), 19
White Dove (variations), 52

Spring
Many flowers work for this theme, but these are particularly spring-like
Apple Tree Charm Tack, 41
Breezy Blossom, 47
Butterfly Garden, 74
Feathers & Flowers, 44
Floating Lily, 55
Flower of Youth, 63
Friendship Blossoms, 22
Garden Party, 25
Lemon Twist, 42
Love's Bloom, 56
Petite Daisy, 21
Shasta Daisy, 21
Spring Promise, 43
Strawberry Fields, 16

Summer Leaves, 19
Sunshine, 45
Tulip, 13

Abstract Look
Fanciful Star, 38
Lotus Bud, 75
Monarch, 78
Star Bound (variations), 32
White Dove, 52

Combinations
April Love with
 Cupid's Arrow, 66
Bunting & Bows
 with Poinsettia, 77
Floating Clouds & Stars
 with Sunshine, 45
Furrow Cable with Tulip, 64
Furrow Cable with
 Flower of Youth, 64
Leaf Trail with
 Breezy Blossom, 28
Leaf Trail with Bell Blossom, 28
Summer Leaves with
 Breezy Blossom, 19

Celtic/Cable Look
Avalon, 17
Continuous Cable, 81
Furrow Cable, 64–65
Irish Cable, 54
Lacy Lock, 53
Lady Luck, 11
Furrow Cable, 64–65

Hawaiian Look
Festive Touch, 18
Scotch Thistle, 51

Winter
Crystal Star, 47
Snowflake Charm Tack, 30

Holiday
Bunting & Bows, 77
Crystal Star, 47
Gift Wrap, 30–31
Milky Way, 75
Pie Charm Tack, 53
Poinsettia, 76
Reindeer Charm Tack, 30
Ribbon Reel, 81
Snowflake Charm Tack, 30
Spinning Top Charm Tack, 53

Southwestern Look
Chinook, 36
Cupid's Arrow, 57
Fond Memories, 58
Palace Steps, 35
Thunderbird, 20
Whirlwind, 79

Stars
Fanciful Star, 38
Floating Clouds & Stars, 45
Mariner's Star, 40
Milky Way, 75
Ring of Stars, 46
Star Bound, 32

Sky
Autumn Breeze, 80
Crystal Star, 47
Floating Clouds & Stars, 45
Milky Way, 75
Snowflake Charm Tack, 30
Soaring Bird, 70
Star Bound, 32
Sunshine, 45

Swirls and Waves
Autumn Breeze, 80
Brocade (variations), 39
Cloverleaf, 72
Chinook, 36
Lacy Lock, 53
Leaf Cable, 26
Swirl Charm Tack, 53
Twirlaway, 59
Whirlwind, 79
Windswept, 62

Woven Look
Avalon, 17
Furrow Cable, 64–65
Lady Luck, 11
Mariner's Star, 40

Continuous-Line Patterns
Amish Traditions, 34
Apple Tree Charm Tack, 41
Bell Blossom, 22
Butterfly Charm Tack, 25
Butterfly Garden, 74
Castle Charm Tack, 24
Catch of the Day, 42
Chinook, 36
Cloverleaf, 72
Coleus Leaf, 24
Coventry, 69
Cow Charm Tack, 71
Crystal Star, 47
Double Heart Charm Tack, 25
Fanciful Star (variation), 38
Festive Touch (border), 18
Feathered Wreath (variations), 23
Goose Charm Tack, 71
Hearts Aflutter, 80
Hedgerow, 71
Kite Charm Tack, 24
Lacy Lock, 53
Lantern Lily, 12
Leaf Cable, 26

Leaf Trail, 28
Milky Way, 75
Monarch, 78
Palace Steps, 35
Pie Charm Tack, 53
Rabbit Charm Tack, 54
Reindeer Charm Tack, 30
Snowflake Charm Tack, 30
Soaring Bird, 70
Spinning Top Charm Tack, 53
Spring Promise, 43
Star Bound, 32
Summer Leaves, 19
Sundae Surprise (variation), 29
Sunshine, 45
Swirl Charm Tack, 53
Turtle Charm Tack, 54
Twins Charm Tack, 32
Twirlaway, 59
Whirlabout (variation), 14
Whirlwind, 79
White Dove, 52
Windswept, 62

Alphabetical Index
Amish Traditions, 34–35
Apple Tree Charm Tack, 41
April Love, 66
Autumn Breeze, 80
Avalon, 17
Bell Blossom, 22
Breezy Blossom, 47
Brocade, 39
Bunting & Bows, 77
Butterflies, 50
Butterfly Charm Tack, 25
Butterfly Garden, 74
Camellia, 37
Castle Charm Tack, 24
Catch of the Day, 42
Chinook, 36
Cloverleaf, 72
Coleus Leaf, 24
Continuous Cable, 81
Corona, 27
Coventry, 68–69
Cow Charm Tack, 71
Crystal Star, 47
Cupid's Arrow, 57
Double Feather Wreath, 73
Double Heart Charm Tack, 25
Fanciful Star, 38
Feathered Wreath, 23
Feathers & Flowers, 44
Feather Spray, 60–61
Festive Touch, 18–19
First Bloom, 15
Floating Clouds & Stars, 45
Floating Lily, 55
Flower of Youth, 63
Fond Memories, 58

Friendship Blossoms, 22
Furrow Cable, 64–65
Garden Party, 25
Gift Wrap, 30–31
Goose Charm Tack, 71
Hearts Aflutter, 80
Hearts in Bloom, 48–49
Hedgerow, 71
Irish Cable, 54
Ivy, 67
Kite Charm Tack, 24
Lacy Lock, 53
Lady Luck, 11
Lantern Lily, 12
Leaf Cable, 26
Leaf Trail, 28
Lemon Twist, 42
Lida Rose, 10
Lotus Bud, 75
Love's Bloom, 56–57
Mariner's Star, 40–41
Milky Way, 75
Monarch, 78
Palace Steps, 35
Peach Harvest, 78
Petite Daisy, 21
Pie Charm Tack, 53
Poinsettia, 76
Rabbit Charm Tack, 54
Reindeer Charm Tack, 30
Ribbon Reel, 81
Ring of Stars, 46
Rosebush, 79
Scotch Thistle, 50–51
Shasta Daisy, 21
Snowflake Charm Tack, 30
Soaring Bird, 70
Spinning Top Charm Tack, 53
Spring Promise, 43
Star Bound, 32
Strawberry Fields, 16
Summer Leaves, 19
Sunshine, 45
Sundae Surprise, 29
Swirl Charm Tack, 53
Thunderbird, 20
Tulip, 13
Turtle Charm Tack, 54
Twins Charm Tack, 32
Twirlaway, 59
Whirlabout, 14
Whirlwind, 79
White Dove, 52
Wild Rose, 15
Windswept, 62
Zinnia, 33

THE *Quiltmaker* COLLECTION ▪ *Quilting Motifs* ▪ **87**

Circle & Angle Templates

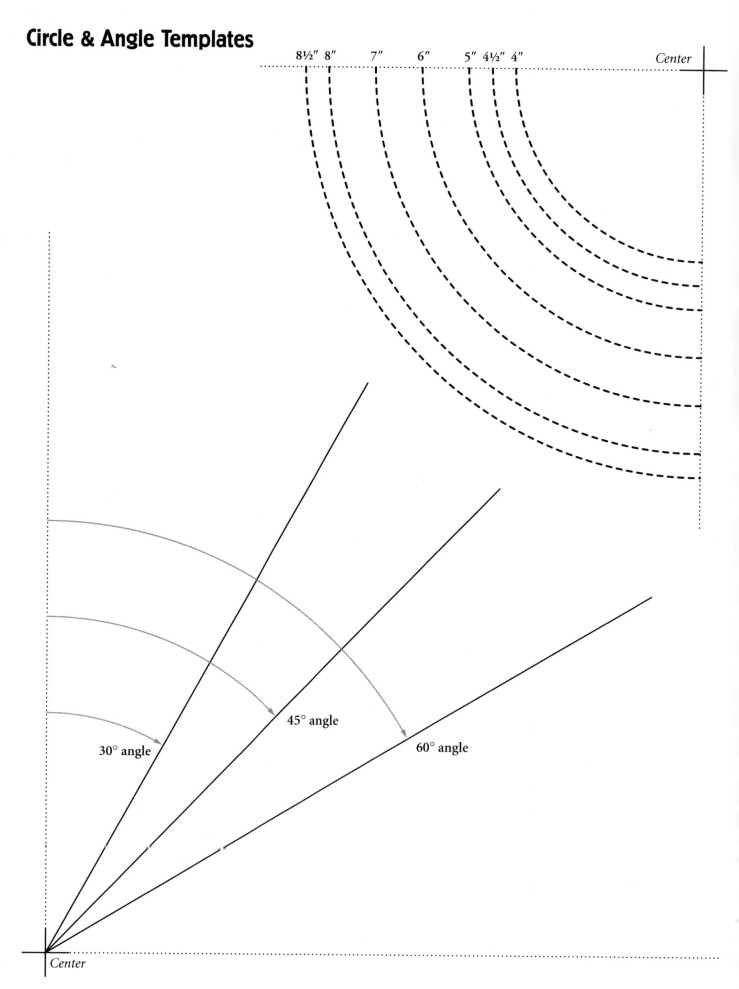

At Quiltmaker
Step-by-Step Patterns, Tips & Techniques

We take great ideas and QUILT them!

QUILTMAKER is written by quilters for quilters!

Every QUILTMAKER issue features 10 or more brand-new, never-before seen patterns and quilting designs. Whether you're a beginner or a professional, whether you're looking for a wall quilt or a queen size comforter—you'll find what you need in QUILTMAKER!

Every issue features:
- *Easy, Step-by-Step Directions*
- *Accurate Yardages*
- *Time-Saving Patterns*
- *Color Options*
- *Custom Quilting Motifs*
- *Quilts in Many Sizes and for All Skill Levels*

Return your Reply Card Today!
We'll start your subscription to QUILTMAKER, giving you a full year of quilt patterns, lessons, tips, and more! If another quilter has already used the attached card, call us today at 1.800.477.6089, or you can also subscribe by writing to QUILTMAKER, PO BOX 58360, Boulder, CO 80322-8360

SUBSCRIBE TODAY!

SAVE UP TO 34%

At Quiltmaker
Step-by-Step Patterns, Tips & Techniques

we take great ideas and QUILT them!

❏ 2 years (12 issues) only $38.98. SAVE 34%

❏ 1 year (6 issues) only $21.98. SAVE 26%

Name (please print) _____

Address _____ Apt. # ____

City _____ State _____ Zip _____

E-mail Address _____

Would you like to receive special e-mail offers from *Quiltmaker* and qualified users of our mailing list? ❏ Yes ❏ No

Send no money now—we'll bill you later!

Please allow 6-8 weeks for delivery of your first issue. Outside U.S., add $10 per year postage. (Includes Canadian GST and HST.) U.S. funds only.

5MOT

SAVE UP TO
34%

BUSINESS REPLY MAIL
FIRST-CLASS MAIL   PERMIT NO 1186   BOULDER, CO

POSTAGE WILL BE PAID BY ADDRESSEE

NO POSTAGE
NECESSARY
IF MAILED IN THE
UNITED STATES

Quiltmaker
Step-by-Step Patterns, Tips & Techniques

P.O. BOX 58358
BOULDER, CO 80323-8358

Enjoy these columns in every issue:

Pattern Parade

Quilt Class

Basic Lessons

Gizmos & Gotta Haves

Sew to Speak

Stitch & Show

Fabric-A-Fair

Quiltmaker's Market

Quiltmaker